W9-AXZ-151

Places In Time

A Kid's Historic Guide to the Changing Names and Places of the World

A Brief Political and Geographic History of

Africa

Where Are... Belgian Congo, Rhodesia, and Kush

Mitchell Lane
PUBLISHERS

P.O. Box 196
Hockessin, Delaware 19707
Visit us on the web: www.mitchelllane.com
Comments? email us: mitchelllane@mitchelllane.com

Places In Time
A Kid's Historic Guide to the Changing Names and Places of the World

Titles in the Series

A Brief Political and Geographic History of . . .

Africa
Where Are Belgian Congo, Rhodesia, and Kush?

Asia
Where Are Saigon, Kampuchea, and Burma?

Europe
Where Are Prussia, Gaul, and the Holy Roman Empire?

Latin America
Where Are Gran Colombia, La Plata, and Dutch Guiana?

The Middle East
Where Are Persia, Babylon, and the Ottoman Empire?

North America
Where Are New France, New Netherland, and New Sweden?

Places In Time
A Kid's Historic Guide to the Changing Names and Places of the World

A Brief Political and Geographic History of

Africa

Where Are... Belgian Congo, Rhodesia, and Kush

John Davenport

Mitchell Lane
PUBLISHERS

P.O. Box 196
Hockessin, Delaware 19707
Visit us on the web: www.mitchelllane.com
Comments? email us: mitchelllane@mitchelllane.com

Printing   1   2   3   4   5   6   7   8   9

Library of Congress Cataloging-in-Publication Data
Davenport, John, 1960–
    A brief political and geographic history of Africa : where are Belgian Congo, Rhodesia, and Kush? / by John Davenport.
        p. cm. — (Places in time : a kid's historic guide to the changing names and places in the world)
    Includes bibliographical references and index.
    ISBN 978-1-58415-624-6 (library bound)
    1. Africa—History—Juvenile literature. 2. Africa—Historical geography—Juvenile literature. I. Title.
DT22.D29 2008
960—dc22

                          2007013175

PHOTO CREDITS: Maps by Jonathan Scott—pp. 6, 7, 18, 25, 28, 35, 38, 45, 48, 55, 58, 65, 68, 75, 78, 88, 97; pp. 10, 42, 43, 47, 52, 52, 60, 61, 62, 67, 70, 71, 72, 74, 76, 83, 91—JupiterImages; p. 11—Fabrizio Demartis/Creative Commons; p. 14—De Agostini/Getty Images; pp. 20, 30, 41, 56, 64—NASA; pp. 21, 22, 32—Barbara Marvis; p. 23—Library of Congress; p. 26—World Heritage; p. 34—British Library/Bibliothèque Nationale, Paris; p. 40—National Maritime Museum; p. 44 (left)—Roger Viollet Collection/Getty Images; p. 44 (right)—DeA Picture Library; pp. 50, 51—WGBH/PBS; p. 54—Jan Derk; p. 73—Hulton Deutsch; p. 80—Richard Knötel; p. 81—German Old Army; p. 82—Creative Commons; p. 85—World War II Pictures in Color; p. 86—Archives.gov; p. 90—U.S. Federal Government; p. 92—Reuters; p. 94—Politique Internationale, Afrique; p. 95—Agence Dalmas; p. 96—Hulton Archive/Getty Images; p. 98—Louise Gubb/Corbis; p. 112—Jennifer Davenport.

PUBLISHER'S NOTE: This story is based on the author's extensive research, which he believes to be accurate. Documentation of such research is contained on page 107.
    The internet sites referenced herein were active as of the publication date. Due to the fleeting nature of some web sites, we cannot guarantee they will all be active when you are reading this book.
    To reflect current usage, we have chosen to use the secular era designations BCE ("before the common era") and CE ("of the common era") instead of the traditional designations BC ("before Christ") and AD (*anno Domini,* "in the year of the Lord").

                                                                PLB

Places In Time

Table of Contents

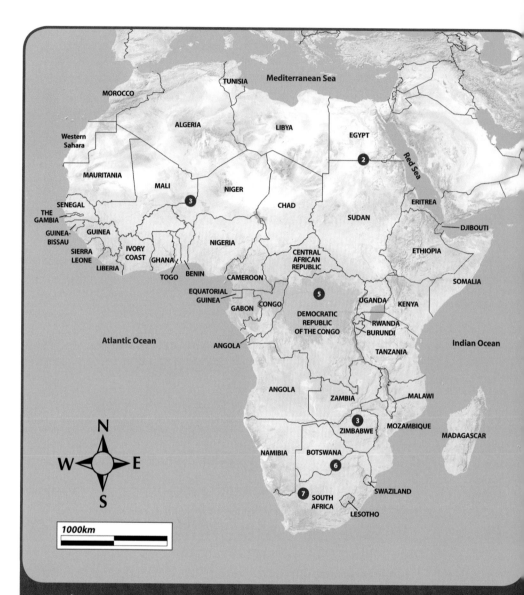

MOROCCO

TUNISIA

Mediterranean Sea

ALGERIA

LIBYA

EGYPT

Red Sea

Western
Sahara

MAURITANIA

MALI

NIGER

CHAD

SUDAN

ERITREA

DJIBOUTI

SENEGAL

THE
GAMBIA

GUINEA-
BISSAU

GUINEA

SIERRA
LEONE

IVORY
COAST

LIBERIA

GHANA

TOGO

BENIN

NIGERIA

CAMEROON

CENTRAL
AFRICAN
REPUBLIC

ETHIOPIA

SOMALIA

EQUATORIAL
GUINEA

GABON

CONGO

DEMOCRATIC
REPUBLIC
OF THE CONGO

UGANDA

KENYA

RWANDA

BURUNDI

Atlantic Ocean

ANGOLA

TANZANIA

Indian Ocean

ANGOLA

ZAMBIA

MALAWI

ZIMBABWE

MOZAMBIQUE

MADAGASCAR

NAMIBIA

BOTSWANA

N

W   E

S

SWAZILAND

SOUTH
AFRICA

LESOTHO

1000km

Use this map to guide your journey through the history of Africa. Each number in red
identifies the chapter in which a particular geographic area is covered. Chapters 1, 4, 8,
and 9 deal more generally with the whole continent.

Introduction

The map of Africa, with its distinctive contours, is familiar to most people. A brief glimpse at the evening news will acquaint even the casual observer with place names such as Egypt, Sudan, the Congo, and Zimbabwe. Global politics, war, and famine draw our attention to these locations. But we tend to forget that Africa is much larger than the points on the map that make it onto our television screens. It is also easily forgotten that Africa is much older than the most recent news. Many places on what was once known as the Dark Continent have disappeared, from maps and from our awareness. Mighty empires have risen and fallen in Africa; great kingdoms have come and gone. City-states have altered the course of history, while entire cultures have emerged only to dissolve in time. Colonies, possessed and exploited by foreigners who cared little for the local people, have appeared and then, seemingly in an instant, vanished. The wisps of memory swirl around Africa as they do no other continent.

Kush, the Belgian Congo, Rhodesia—these places have been erased from modern maps of the world. At one time, they represented the pride and prestige of kings and queens, yet in the twenty-first century, none of these places exist anymore. Kush, the Belgian Congo, and Rhodesia have dissolved into the ages; few know them and even fewer can locate them. Still, their legacies live on. The places they were have become nations we recognize. Changing and shifting, coming in and out of focus, they have survived to this day as places in time.

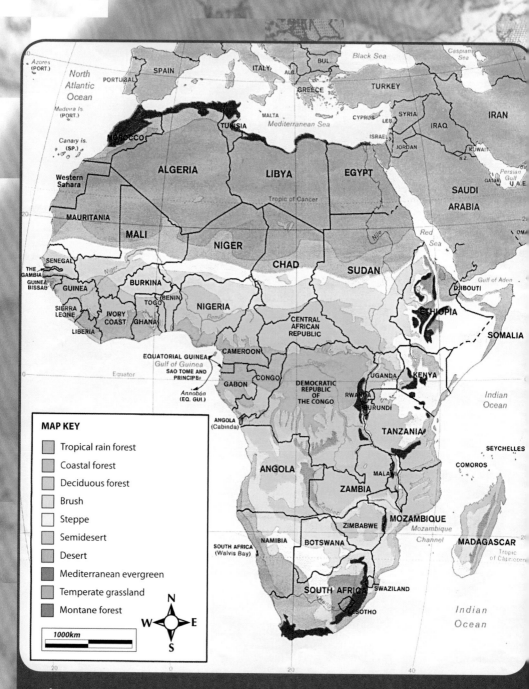

MAP KEY

- Tropical rain forest
- Coastal forest
- Deciduous forest
- Brush
- Steppe
- Semidesert
- Desert
- Mediterranean evergreen
- Temperate grassland
- Montane forest

1000km

N
W ◆ E
S

Africa is a vast continent. Its many regions have different climates and ecosystems—from dry desert to tropical rain forest, from mountain snows to valley grasses.

Strange Things in Strange Places

Every year, tourists visiting Egypt make a special trip to the plain of Giza. There they gaze upon the last remaining structure that is counted among the Seven Wonders of the Ancient World—the Pyramid of Khufu. The Great Pyramids of Giza were built some 4,500 years ago by three Egyptian pharaohs (FARE-ohs), or kings, as massive monuments to their power and glory. Each one sheltered elaborate tomb chambers designed to ensure a regal afterlife for the pharaohs placed inside them. The individual pyramids took perhaps twenty years to construct and involved the labor of over 20,000 workers.

Standing hundreds of feet tall and constructed out of millions of blocks of solid limestone that weigh several tons each, the Great Pyramids are the most easily recognized symbols of an Egyptian culture and society that disappeared long ago. Along with their many gods and the Nile River, which flows just to the east, these pyramids represent everything that the ancient Egyptians held sacred. Yet if a tourist were to get on a boat and sail farther up the azure waters of the Nile from Giza, he or she would make a startling discovery.

Far to the south of the old land of the pharaohs, among the craggy mountains and dusty highlands of a place once called Nubia (NOO-bee-ah), are the remains of 233 pyramids. Built on the dry flatlands surrounding the ruins of ancient cities such as Meroe (mer-oh-WE), these pyramids served many of the same functions as their northern counterparts: They were both religious symbols and monuments to the dead. Although very few tourists ever visit them, these pyramids are

Three monuments to former glories, the Pyramids of Giza stand in the Egyptian desert as reminders of an ancient past. The Pyramid of Khafre (center) is the only one that retains some of the smooth casing stones that sheathed all three. The Great Pyramid, built for Khufu, is the large pyramid on the left.

recognized by scholars as being among the most important archaeological objects in the world. Some of these monuments are so impressive and historically valuable that their location was listed as a World Cultural Heritage Site by the United Nations in 2003.

These well-preserved pyramids dot the landscape of the modern nation of Sudan (soo-DAN) for all to see. They stand as odd replicas of

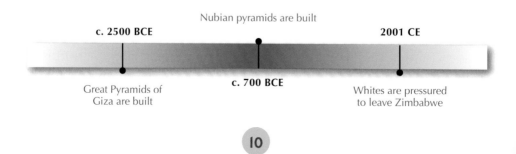

Nubian pyramids are built

c. 2500 BCE

2001 CE

Great Pyramids of
Giza are built

c. 700 BCE

Whites are pressured
to leave Zimbabwe

Less well-known than their counterparts in Egypt are the Sudanese pyramids near the city of Meroe. The Nubians inherited the practice of pyramid building from their northern neighbors.

a building style that died out in its native land, only to be revived centuries later in a faraway place. The Sudanese pyramids are considerably smaller than those in Egypt and have a somewhat different design, but they have survived through time in much better shape. Whereas many Egyptian pyramids other than the three at Giza are in ruins, the ones in Sudan by and large stand intact, some looking as if they have just been built. They have lost none of their original beauty and grace.

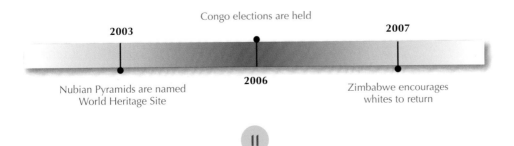

Congo elections are held

2003   2007

2006

Nubian Pyramids are named World Heritage Site

Zimbabwe encourages whites to return

The real question, however, does not concern the Sudanese pyramids' quality or aesthetic value. It is how these ancient peoples came to adopt the practice of pyramid construction in the first place. They were not ethnically related to their northern neighbors. Their religious beliefs and rituals were different. Yet they built pyramids, each standing above Egyptian-style tomb chambers whose dead occupants "were mummified, covered with jewelry and laid to rest in wooden coffins,"[1] just like the ones in Egypt. In another similarity, the tomb antechambers are packed with "piles of fine ceramics, jewels, arms, toilet objects, chests and beds of wood inlaid with ivory."[2]

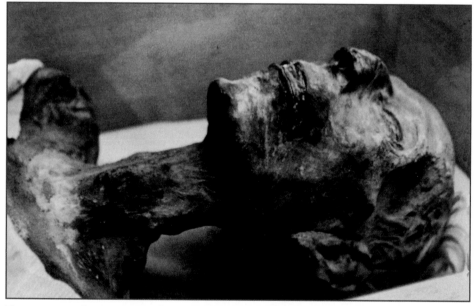

The mummy of Rameses II, who ruled Egypt at its height. He is reputed to have been the biblical pharaoh who refused to let the ancient Hebrews leave Egypt for the promised land.

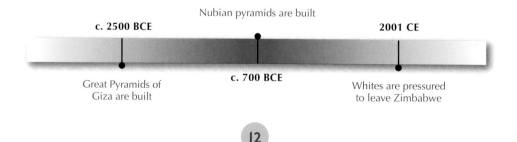

Nubian pyramids are built

c. 2500 BCE

2001 CE

c. 700 BCE

Great Pyramids of
Giza are built

Whites are pressured
to leave Zimbabwe

Following the axis of Africa still farther south, travelers enter the heart of the continent. Lush rain forests cover the land. Misty mountains, teeming with exotic animals and plants, tower above highland valleys and plateaus. Slicing their way to the west, the waters of a mighty river carry with them a name synonymous with central Africa—the Congo. Along its shores and farther inland, people carved out communities and kingdoms, each unique in its social structure, culture, and language. Tribal groups built towns and cities and hunted and cultivated a huge area that reached all the way to the plateaus of south-central Africa. At one point, a powerful kingdom that was renowned as far as Europe emerged.

Yet despite the obvious African culture of the Congo's people, a foreign language holds sway today in government offices and the halls of justice. During the 2006 presidential election, the opposition candidate repeated his slogan everywhere: "Pour La Sécurité, La Justice, et Le Développement" (For Security, Justice, and Development).[3] The official language of the modern Democratic Republic of the Congo is French. And not just French, but French tinged with a Belgian accent. Thousands of miles away from the tiny European country of Belgium, millions of Africans speak its language and elevate it above their own when it comes to government business. The Congo offers an African home to a European tongue.

Farther south still is the country of Zimbabwe. Tracing its proud lineage back to the ancient kingdom of Great Zimbabwe, known famously for its magnificent walled cities, this modern nation could not be more African. Its capital city, Harare, is among Africa's largest. Zimbabwe's second major metropolis, Bulawayo, was once the center of a sprawling kingdom that dominated the region for centuries.

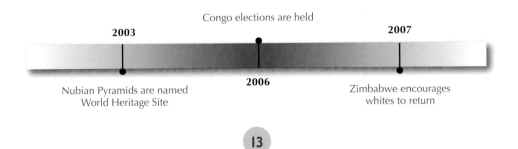

Congo elections are held

2003   2007

2006

Nubian Pyramids are named
World Heritage Site

Zimbabwe encourages
whites to return

Here, however, in one of the continent's major states, in 2007 a black government was set to welcome back farmers who were displaced by an official program to rid the country of a hated minority group. The members of that group are both Zimbabwean and white. Almost 5,000 white farmers tilled the soil of Zimbabwe in 2001; six years later, a mere 600 remained. By that time, the government of President Robert Mugabe (moo-GAH-bee) was trying to keep those remaining whites in Zimbabwe while actively working to lure the

Ringed by thick walls, the city of Great Zimbabwe was the center of an important kingdom in southern Africa. Its architecture was far more advanced than that of the local villagers who lived outside the walls.

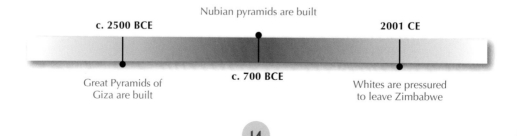

Nubian pyramids are built

c. 2500 BCE

2001 CE

Great Pyramids of
Giza are built

c. 700 BCE

Whites are pressured
to leave Zimbabwe

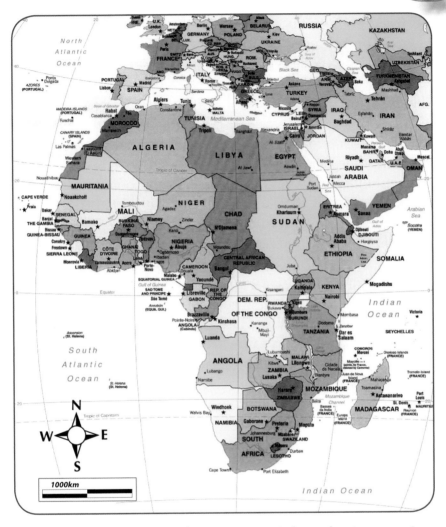

Modern Africa is a continent of many nations. Each one has its own unique culture and traditions. The boundaries of some areas, such as Western Sahara, are still in dispute.

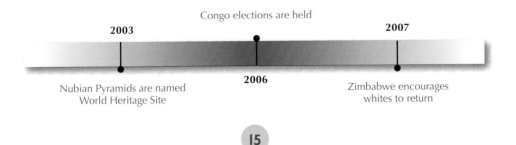

Congo elections are held

2003

2007

Nubian Pyramids are named World Heritage Site

2006

Zimbabwe encourages whites to return

others back home. The same man who once defiantly declared that Zimbabwe belonged exclusively to blacks "by natural and legal right . . . by legacy"[4] now hoped to get his country's white citizens back.

There were many reasons for this renewed interest in a multiracial Zimbabwe. The whites possessed many needed skills—especially in the area of agriculture, an economic sector that has struggled in terms of output. But the question that begs to be answered is how so many white people came to live in a black African country to begin with, and why, when asked, they considered themselves to be Zimbabwean rather than European. Even those whites who rejected the government's calls to return refused to leave Africa, preferring to move to nearby Zambia or Mozambique instead. Why?

Monumental structures, languages, and racial groups, all out of place. Things and people are where they logically should not be in Africa. As is so often the case, fascinating stories reaching back into the past explain how all this came to be. These are tales of empire and conquest, of heroism and villainy, tales that involve a wide-ranging cast of famous and infamous characters. The stories span a long period of time and span the gulfs among several continents.

Understanding and appreciating them, however, does require a bit of time travel. In other words, to firmly grasp the history of Africa and, in particular, places such as those that once occupied the geographical spaces currently held by Sudan, the Democratic Republic of the Congo, and Zimbabwe, people must journey quite a way back and visit many diverse and exciting places in time.

White Zimbabwe

The tension between white and black Africans in Zimbabwe is far from uncommon. Robert Mugabe's contradictory policy of first driving out and then later welcoming back white farmers reflects a conflict unique to Africa. Despite the fact that many whites have lived in Africa for generations, black Africans often do not accept their white neighbors and remain suspicious about white intentions. They see Africa as a black land that unfortunately harbors a minority of white interlopers.

Many blacks, especially in places like Zimbabwe, feel that whites have not suffered historically as blacks have, nor do they have any right to claim an African heritage. They view confiscating the property of whites or expelling them altogether as justified. As one black Zimbabwean wrote, most whites consider Africa to be "their motherland," but they should still "feel the pain of loss, too. What did they think they were doing when they took the lands of Africans in the first place?"[5]

White Africans, on the other hand, feel that the continent is just as much theirs as anyone else's. Over four and a half million whites live in South Africa, with many more in Kenya, Tanzania, Mozambique, Senegal, Ivory Coast, Zambia, Nigeria, and Zimbabwe. These people have strong family ties to Africa that in some cases reach back for centuries. Most white Africans have never lived anywhere else. The resentment of the black majority, the taking of their lands or businesses, and the constant threat of being chased from their homes hurt deeply.

Whites understand why they are looked down upon and feared, but they claim they can contribute to the future of Africa in important ways. Scholar Robert Rorberg has argued, "There is a role for whites in the new 21st-century Africa,"[6] and leaders such as Mugabe seem to be agreeing, however grudgingly. To Stuart Carlisle, the white captain of a Zimbabwean champion cricket team, Africa is home. "I'm not denying that things are tough," Carlisle said, "but [Zimbabwe is] where I was born, I love the country and I don't see why I should move."[7]

Stuart Carlisle playing cricket for Zimbabwe

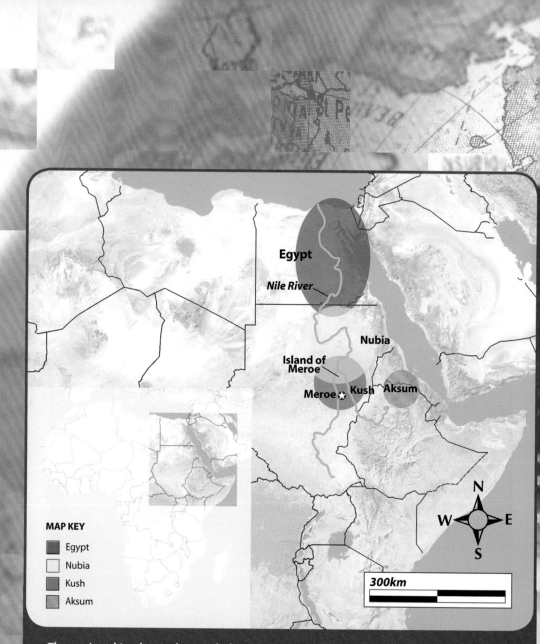

Egypt

Nile River

Nubia

Island of Meroe

Meroe ☆ **Kush** **Aksum**

MAP KEY

Egypt

Nubia

Kush

Aksum

N
W E
S

300km

The ancient kingdoms clustered along or near the Nile River to take advantage of its life-giving waters. Each one prospered through agriculture and trade. The Island of Meroe was a region between the White Nile, Blue Nile, and Atbara rivers.

Chapter 2

From Nubia to Kush

The ancient Greek historian Herodotus called Egypt "the gift of the Nile." He meant that the crystal blue waters of the Nile River gave the world one of its great treasures, the land and people of Egypt. And a fabulous gift it was. Stretching hundreds of miles in length but at points only a few miles wide, ancient Egypt followed the graceful curves of the Nile, and crossed the deserts and mountains of north-eastern Africa. Blessed with dark, rich soil that the Nile provided during its annual floods, Egypt produced enough food to feed its people and maintain a thriving export market. Yet Egypt had to import many other necessities.

These imports came from just about everywhere in the ancient Near East. Wood, for example, was imported from the area around modern Lebanon; precious gemstones came from Mesopotamia and the land that would someday become Afghanistan. Wine and olive oil came from faraway places like Crete and the other Greek islands. Some of the most valuable products, however—such as gold, ivory, ostrich feathers, and ebony wood—came from nearby Nubia.

Beginning in the Old Kingdom period (c. 2695–2195 BCE), Egyptian pharaohs launched raids into Nubia to either capture trade goods outright or force the Nubians to supply them in an arrangement known as tribute. Tribute was a form of blackmail in which one people defeated another group in war and then demanded that they pay them in goods on a yearly basis. The tribute demanded by the victorious Egyptians included everything from gold and dogs to slaves. One royal

Photographed from many miles up in space, the Nile appears as a blue ribbon among the browns and dusty yellows of the North African desert. Bright green fields flank the life-giving waters of the Nile.

officer, who led an expedition to Nubia around the year 2278 BCE, gloated that it took him only seven months to go south and come back with "all kinds of beautiful and rare gifts." He noted that he "was praised for it very greatly."[1]

For centuries, the Egyptians sent expeditions into Nubia to squeeze tribute. Finally, around the beginning of the New Kingdom period of Egyptian history (c. 1535–1050 BCE), the Egyptians moved into Nubia to stay; they made the entire land a colony of the Egyptian Empire. The Egyptian occupation of Nubia ensured that valuable products flowed uninterrupted from central Africa and Nubia into Egypt.

It also guaranteed the movement of ideas and customs southward into Nubia. These included Egyptian religious beliefs and practices and elements of the Egyptian language (especially hieroglyphic writing). Perhaps most important, at least for modern historians and archaeologists,

c. 2695–c. 2195 BCE

New Kingdom period

1050 BCE

Old Kingdom period

c. 1535–c. 1050 BCE

Nubia is freed

Egyptian art and architecture traveled up the Nile to Nubia. Temples, sphinxes, and pyramids became common features on the Nubian landscape. All represented a "cultural exchange [that] was almost entirely a one-way process"[2]—a thorough Egyptianization of Nubia that would leave a lasting imprint on the future.

One of the first to invent writing, the Egyptians relied on a form called hieroglyphics, a type of picture writing. Only in the early nineteenth century, when the French translated the ancient text, did it become possible to read the words of ancient Egypt.

Egypt ruled Nubia for nearly five hundred years, taking its trade goods and leaving behind the culture of the pharaohs. Then, around 1050 BCE, New Kingdom Egypt collapsed, freeing Nubia. With their former overlords gone, the Nubians created their own kingdom. Centered on the city of Napata (NAH-puh-tuh), the Nubians built a state that combined economic and military power. It was known as Kush (or Cush).

By the mid-eighth century BCE, the Kushites, as the Nubians were now called, were strong enough to push northward. In about 730 BCE, the Kushites took over Egypt and turned the tables on their former masters. Nubian kings sat on the Egyptian throne, dressing and giving orders as pharaohs, and running Egypt as part of their own realm.

Trouble was on the horizon, trouble in the form of a ferocious warrior people called the Assyrians (uh-SEE-ree-uns), who were described

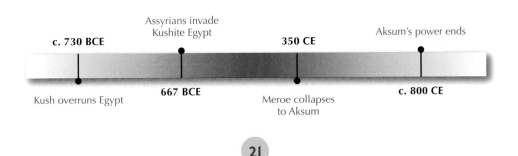

c. 730 BCE

Kush overruns Egypt

667 BCE

Assyrians invade Kushite Egypt

Meroe collapses to Aksum

350 CE

Aksum's power ends

c. 800 CE

Part human, part lion, sphinxes were guardian creatures in Egyptian religion. The Great Sphinx, above, protects the pyramid of Khafre.

at the time as being like a "bird of prey [that] filled the world with blood."[3] Storming out of their Mesopotamian homeland around 900 BCE, the Assyrians conquered all before them. By the early seventh century BCE, their armies stood poised to invade Egypt. The Kushites tried to defend their adopted land, but the Assyrians were too strong. They forced the Kushites to withdraw and reestablish themselves at the city of Meroe.

c. 2695–
c. 2195 BCE

New Kingdom period

1050 BCE

Old Kingdom period

c. 1535–
c. 1050 BCE

Nubia is freed

An Egyptian temple in Nubia. Ancient Nubia and Egypt grew together. At many points, their histories intersected.

Meroe sat on land that formed a broad peninsula between the southern reaches of the Nile and the smaller Atbara River to the east. This peninsula led people to call the entire area around the new Kushite capital "the Island of Meroe." True island or not, Meroe had distinct advantages over Napata. Great quantities of iron ore were located there. Combined with an abundant supply of wood, the ore allowed a thriving iron industry to grow up around Meroe.

The climate was also wetter than it was farther north. More rain translated into larger grain harvests and an expanding supply of food

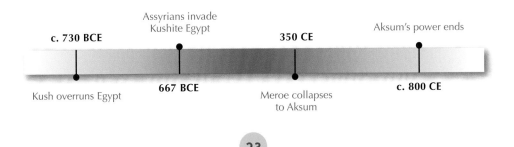

Assyrians invade
Kushite Egypt

c. 730 BCE   350 CE   Aksum's power ends

Kush overruns Egypt   667 BCE   Meroe collapses   c. 800 CE
                                       to Aksum

for the growing population. Because it was closer than Egypt to the Red Sea, Meroe could function as a bustling center of trade and business. Meroe's flat plain allowed the Kushite kings to build their stunning pyramids as testaments to their regal authority and reminders of their enduring connections to ancient Egypt.

Life was good at Meroe, at least until the first few centuries of the Common Era. Kush's iron industry consumed large amounts of wood to stoke the furnaces where iron was smelted. Over time, the forests of Kush vanished, and without any trees to burn, the iron industry ceased to exist. Worse yet, soil erosion whisked away the topsoil needed for successful agriculture. Food shortages, followed by famine, became routine. Coupled with the disappearance of trade, Meroe became hungry and poor. Just as Meroe was at its weakest, the city was attacked by the armies of a rising city-state to its southeast, the kingdom of Aksum (ahk-SOOM). In 350 CE, weakened beyond repair, Meroe fell.

Aksum took over where the Kushites had left off. They were, however, somewhat different from the Kushites and Nubians before them. One difference was that the Aksumites had abandoned their old religion with many gods and adopted Christianity around the time they conquered Meroe. Aided by their location on the Red Sea, they also engaged in trade to an extent Meroe would have envied. Aksum primarily exported ivory, slaves, and resins such as frankincense and myrrh; among other things, it imported gold, silver, olive oil, and wine.

Aksum resembled Nubia, though, in its appetite for monumental construction, in this case towering obelisks known as stelae (STEH-lee). Rising up like stone knife blades, the highest were nearly 100 feet

c. 2695–
c. 2195 BCE

New Kingdom period

1050 BCE

Old Kingdom period

c. 1535–
c. 1050 BCE

Nubia is freed

tall and weighed hundreds of tons. They were elaborately decorated and chiseled out of solid stone. The largest stela, scholars have determined, was "probably the largest single block of stone ever quarried, carved and set up in the ancient world."[4]

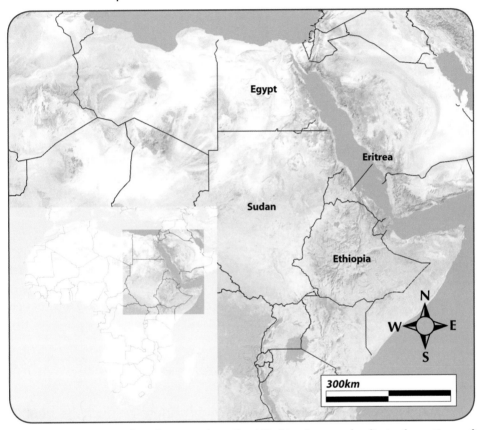

Ancient and modern Africa live together. The Nile kingdoms today lie in the nations of Egypt, Sudan, Eritrea, and Ethiopia.

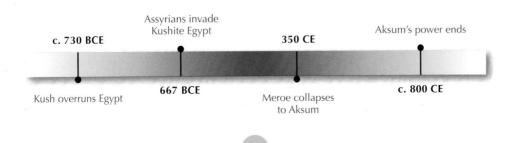

The ancient city of Aksum carried on the Egyptian tradition of monumental architecture. The Aksumite people created huge obelisks, called stelae, as testaments to their power.

Aksum resembled Meroe in one unfortunate respect: Its people treated the environment very harshly and without regard for the future. Once again, deforestation and overfarming led to hunger and industrial decay. Trade, which had always been central to the Aksumite economy, withered away to nothing. By the ninth century, Aksum was gone. Its disappearance cut a connection that stretched back as far as the pharaohs of Egypt. As Aksum faded, so did the legacies of Kush and Nubia.

Nubia and Lake Nasser

During the long history of ancient Egypt, Nubia was often under the threat of Egyptian raids, invasions, and domination. Nubia's modern counterpart is under Egyptian water, at least its northern areas. What was once known as Lower Nubia now lies beneath a massive man-made body of water called Lake Nasser, which was created in 1964 as a result of the construction of the immense Aswan High Dam.

Vast amounts of water are stored in the massive reservoir known as Lake Nasser. Built to control the Nile floods, the lake is named for modern Egypt's founder, Gamal Abdel Nasser.

The dam itself was the crowning achievement of the Egyptian president at the time, Gamal Abdel Nasser. Nasser wanted to harness the Nile to make life better for his people and to place his name among the great leaders of Egyptian history. Nasser, like all Egyptians, viewed the Nile River as the heart of Egyptian life and culture. The Nile's annual floods had watered and fertilized the soil of Egypt for thousands of years, allowing the desert to bloom.

President Gamal Abdel Nasser wanted modern Egypt to be as great as its ancient namesake. Damming the Nile River was his attempt to create a monument to his rule as lasting as those built by the kings and pharaohs of old.

Sometimes, though, the Nile stubbornly refused to overflow its banks, leading to famine. On other occasions, the flooding was excessive, destroying crops and endangering people. Nasser sought to manipulate the river's flow and, at the same time, generate enough electrical power to help Egypt rapidly modernize. The president saw himself as the master of the Nile, the man who would bring his backward land into the twentieth century. The Aswan High Dam was his solution.

Taking ten years to build, the dam blocked the flow of the Nile, backing up its waters into what had been Lower Nubia. Hurriedly evacuating over 90,000 ethnic Nubians from their homes, the Egyptians once again invaded Nubia, this time with billions of gallons of water. A region that had once produced great kings and a vibrant civilization was inundated. Unfortunately for Nasser, he never got to see his grand project come to its completion. He died in 1970, just before the Aswan High Dam became operational.

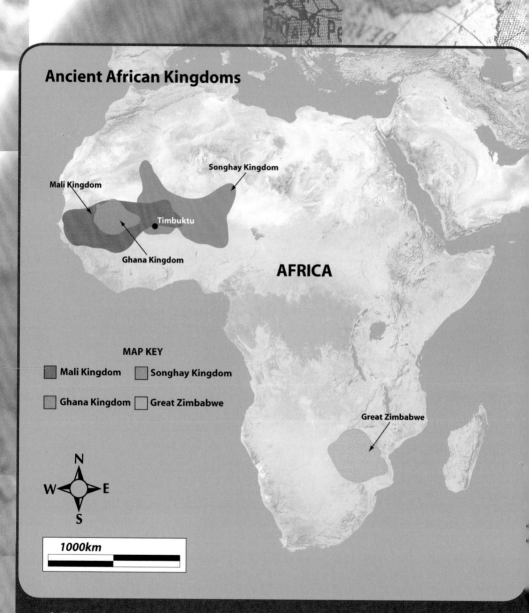

Ancient African Kingdoms

Mali Kingdom

Songhay Kingdom

Timbuktu

Ghana Kingdom

AFRICA

MAP KEY

Mali Kingdom

Songhay Kingdom

Ghana Kingdom

Great Zimbabwe

Great Zimbabwe

N
W E
S

1000km

Of all the African kingdoms and empires, three of the most important were located in West Africa. Ghana, Mali, and Songhay functioned as political and economic centers for a vast territory that covered thousands of square miles.

Chapter 3

Africa for Africans

The centuries that lay between the fall of Aksum and Africa's initial contact with early modern Europe represented a period of immense change and rapid development. Kingdoms rose and fell, populations shifted geographically, new religions emerged, and language groups spread into new areas. Africa certainly was not cut off or isolated from the rest of the world, but no foreign power determined its course of development. Nor did any outside elements exploit the continent for their own benefit. From roughly the ninth to the fifteenth centuries, for the most part Africa grew and progressed on its own. It was truly a time when Africa was for Africans.

Only in terms of religion did the world beyond Africa intrude. In the seventh century, arguably the most important event in the history of Africa since the rise of ancient Egypt took place—the arrival of Islam from the Middle East. Born in Arabia in the early seventh century, Islam became Africa's second monotheistic religion. It complemented Christianity, which had taken hold in Aksum several centuries earlier.

After sweeping over Egypt, Islam spread westward along the coast of North Africa, absorbing local peoples and cultures. By the ninth century, Muslims were in control there. They soon established relations with the long-settled agricultural societies of West Africa, chief among them the Soninke (sah-NIN-kee).

The Soninke were originally farming folk, who very early recognized that they sat squarely between two regions holding large reserves of perhaps the most valuable commodities in the world at the time, gold and salt. Gold, found in abundance in central Africa, had been coveted for millennia as a symbol of power and prosperity. Salt, a vital dietary mineral as well as a key ingredient in drying and preserving meats, covered the ground for thousands of square miles in the western Sahara. The Soninke soon dominated the trade routes along which gold moved northward in exchange for salt coming the other way.

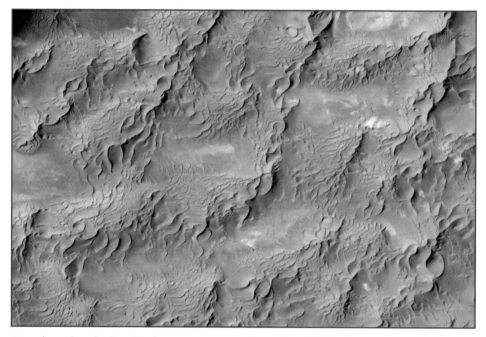

Seen from hundreds of miles out in space, the Sahara looks like a blanket of yellow-brown sand. Much of its western expanse also contains layers of salt.

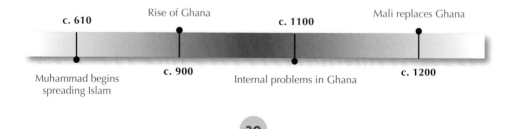

Rise of Ghana

c. 610

c. 1100

Mali replaces Ghana

c. 900

c. 1200

Muhammad begins
spreading Islam

Internal problems in Ghana

This advantageous position made it possible for the Soninke to create the kingdom of Ghana (GAH-nah), the first of three wealthy and influential kingdoms that ruled over West Africa between the ninth and the fifteenth centuries. Ghana originated sometime around the mid-eighth century. It thrived by managing and taxing the gold and salt exchange. A Muslim writer in the tenth century saw so much gold coming from there that he assumed, in "the country of Ghana, gold grows in the sand as carrots do."[1]

Sitting in lavishly furnished palaces, its kings and court officials soon converted to the Islamic faith brought southward by the Muslim salt traders. While this reinforced the economic ties between Ghana and the Muslim north, it had the effect of driving a wedge between Ghana's ruling elite and the people they governed, who persisted in traditional spiritual practices. Social tensions rose.

At the same time, small but intense regional wars broke out between various Soninke factions and between the ruling Soninke and their subject peoples, such as the Malinke (mah-LING-kee). While conflict undermined Ghana socially, changes in the gold market that shifted the best trade routes away from Ghana ruined the kingdom's economy. To make matters worse, efforts to grow enough food to feed an expanding population exhausted the soil and led to supply problems and environmental destruction.

Under such pressures, Ghana could not hold up. It slowly began dissolving into a mass of tiny states. These eventually re-formed in about 1200 under Malinke leadership into the empire of Mali (MAH-lee), Africa's first true empire since the New Kingdom pharaohs ruled Egypt. Born out of the fires of war with the southern Soninke, the

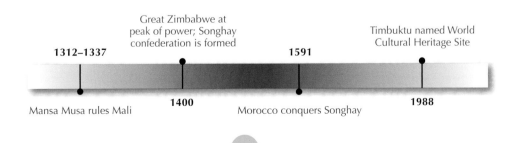

Great Zimbabwe at peak of power; Songhay confederation is formed

1312–1337

1591

Timbuktu named World Cultural Heritage Site

1400

1988

Mansa Musa rules Mali

Morocco conquers Songhay

Malinke state was very similar to Ghana economically. It relied almost exclusively on the gold trade, supported by an agricultural base. The farmers of Mali grew the sorghum, millet, and rice that fed the crafts-people and merchants who made the empire rich. Meanwhile, the revenue from the gold trade allowed Mali to sustain a large royal court, an extensive bureaucracy, and West Africa's largest army.

Mali reached the peak of its power in the fourteenth century. The empire was centered in the legendary city of Timbuktu. Located on the

Islam is often thought of as a Middle Eastern religion. Yet the Djinguereber Mosque, in the ancient city of Timbuktu, demonstrates the power of the Muslim faith in west-central Africa.

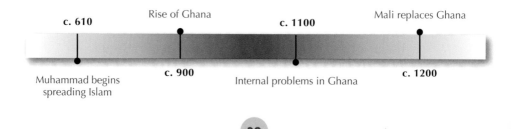

c. 610   Rise of Ghana   c. 1100   Mali replaces Ghana

Muhammad begins spreading Islam   c. 900   Internal problems in Ghana   c. 1200

Niger River, Timbuktu was so historically important in the gold and salt trade that it became a World Cultural Heritage Site in 1988. The empire's wealth was unsurpassed, and direct rule extended from the Atlantic Ocean to what is today the country of Niger.

Mali's rulers were some of the most famous in Africa at the time. They were also fair. An Arab visitor reported that, despite their unquestioned authority, the emperors of Mali were "seldom unjust, and have a greater abhorrence of injustice than any other people."[2]

They were fabulously rich. One of them, Mansa Musa, who ruled from 1312 to 1337, made an extravagant show of his wealth when he traveled to Mecca in 1324 on the hajj (HAHJ), the trip to Islam's holy city expected of all Muslims. In Egypt, he gave away so much gold that prices for the precious metal plummeted during his stay.

Yet strong rulers such as Mansa Musa became fewer as time went on. Around 1400, a series of weak emperors held the throne; the empire stalled under their rule and began to decline. The various people who had lived within Mali's imperial borders soon went their own way.

Some formed themselves into a new confederation that grew into the empire of Songhay. Songhay kings created an efficient government and an economy that flourished on the exchange of gold, kola nuts, and slaves. Songhay grew rapidly, and its reach extended even farther than its predecessors.

The same problems that had doomed Ghana and Mali cropped up. Songhay's ruling class, for example, tried to exercise control over a diverse range of subject peoples, few of whom shared their leaders' devotion to Islam. Agricultural output fell dramatically as Songhay's farmers stripped the soil of nutrients in their effort to grow more crops.

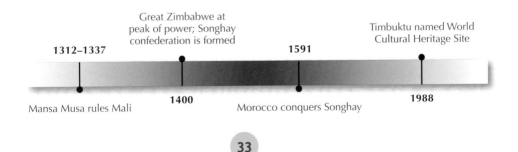

Great Zimbabwe at peak of power; Songhay confederation is formed

Timbuktu named World Cultural Heritage Site

1312–1337

1591

1400

1988

Mansa Musa rules Mali

Morocco conquers Songhay

Trade routes shifted once again, this time toward the Atlantic coast where newly arrived Europeans eagerly waited to purchase African products. Worse still, fierce enemies rose up on Songhay's borders. One of these, Morocco, finally launched an invasion of Songhay in 1591 and erased it from the map. The last of the great West African kingdoms was no more.

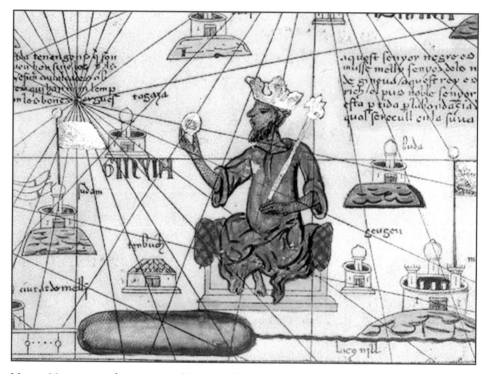

Mansa Musa was a king among kings in Africa, and a just and effective ruler. The gold ornament and golden scepter he holds testify to his fabulous wealth.

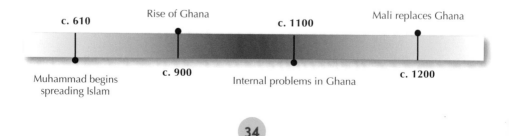

c. 610

Rise of Ghana

c. 1100

Mali replaces Ghana

Muhammad begins spreading Islam

c. 900

Internal problems in Ghana

c. 1200

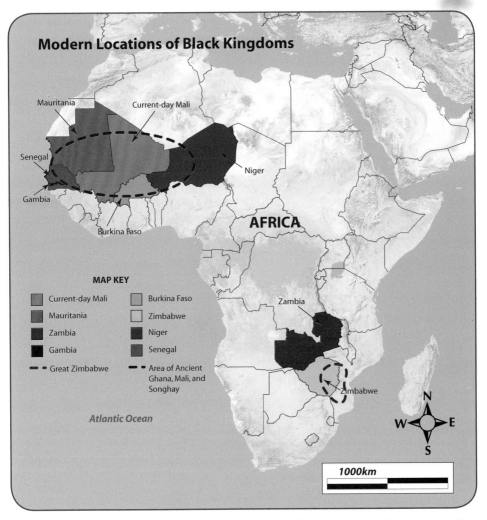

Modern Locations of Black Kingdoms

Mauritania

Current-day Mali

Senegal

Gambia

Burkina Faso

Niger

AFRICA

MAP KEY

- Current-day Mali
- Mauritania
- Zambia
- Gambia
- Burkina Faso
- Zimbabwe
- Niger
- Senegal
- – – Great Zimbabwe
- – – Area of Ancient Ghana, Mali, and Songhay

Atlantic Ocean

Zambia

Zimbabwe

N
W — E
S

1000km

The West African kingdoms and Great Zimbabwe might be gone, but their legacies live on in the modern world. The areas they either ruled or influenced are now the modern nations of Mauritania, Mali, Niger, Burkina Faso, Zambia, and Zimbabwe.

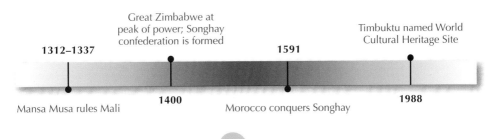

Great Zimbabwe at
peak of power; Songhay
confederation is formed

Timbuktu named World
Cultural Heritage Site

1312–1337

1591

1400

1988

Mansa Musa rules Mali

Morocco conquers Songhay

Far to the south, a similar pattern of rise and fall characterized the history of the Shona (SHOW-nah) kingdom of Great Zimbabwe. Remembered for its distinctive architecture, Great Zimbabwe took its name from the construction techniques its people employed. *Zimbabwe*, in the Shona language, literally means "stone buildings," a reference to the massive walled compounds the Zimbabweans constructed for their rulers. These were the largest structures in Africa south of the pyramids. From these fortress-like palaces, the Shona kings created a state that lay between the Limpopo and Zambezi Rivers. They relied on an economy based on cattle raising and trade in craft products such as jewelry to support a population that grew to at least 11,000 by the late fourteenth century. Merchants from Great Zimbabwe exported iron to, and imported luxury goods from, places as far away as Persia, India, and even China.

Once again, success had its price. The people of Great Zimbabwe did not take care of the environment. They worked the soil too hard, exhausting it. They cut down most of their forests to supply firewood for the iron industry. Trade evaporated and royal power disintegrated. By 1450, Great Zimbabwe had ceased to exist. Its people broke up into small groups and moved away from the stone buildings that had defined them for two hundred years.

Like its northern counterparts, Great Zimbabwe had been an African kingdom for Africans. During its existence, however, newcomers had begun landing on the continent's shores—Europeans who came to trade, colonize, and exploit. The next five hundred years would belong to them.

Islam in Africa

In the early seventh century, Islam swept into Africa. As it spread westward to the shores of the Atlantic Ocean and southward across the burning sands of the Sahara, it opened a rift among the peoples of Africa by effectively cutting the continent in two. Because the great Sahara made travel so difficult, Islam extended its African range only to the desert's southern boundary. The immense swaths of highland rain forests and mountains that girded central Africa remained out of Islam's reach, as did the plateaus, grasslands, and arid plains of southern Africa. Along the East African coast, Muslim beliefs and customs often took hold, but that was only because of the extensive trade connection that existed between East African port cities and Arab lands to the north.

The expansion of Islam into West Africa and along the eastern coast of the continent began about 300 years after the religion had arrived in North Africa. Today, the Muslim call to prayer can be heard five times a day in countries as far south as Nigeria and Mozambique.

The split remains to this day. Across North Africa, Islam is the preeminent religion and the dominant influence in social, cultural, and political life. Muslim Africa begins in Egypt and reaches across the continent to Morocco. Libya, Algeria, and Tunisia are all majority-Muslim states. The Islamic countries of the north include Mali and Mauritania; in the east, Somalia is solidly Muslim.

Moving southward from the Sahara and its borderlands, the age-old rift appears. In places like Chad, Sudan, Nigeria, and the southern coast of West Africa, Islam blends with other belief systems. Muslims often hold sway in the northern areas of these countries, while Christianity and indigenous religions are prevalent in the southern parts. Continuing on to central and southern Africa, a region stretching through the Democratic Republic of the Congo, Zambia, and Zimbabwe into Angola, Namibia, Mozambique, and South Africa, Islam fades away. Modern Africa is divided, then, by a line drawn over a thousand years ago that connects the present with places and people of the past.

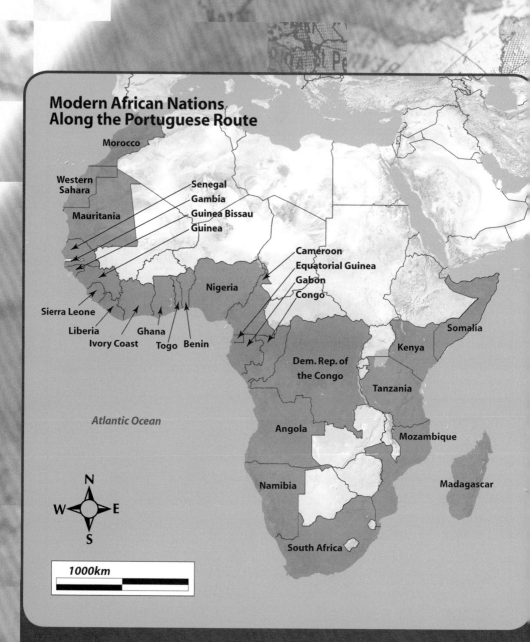

Modern African Nations Along the Portuguese Route

Morocco

Western Sahara

Mauritania

Senegal
Gambia
Guinea Bissau
Guinea

Cameroon
Equatorial Guinea
Gabon
Congo

Nigeria

Sierra Leone

Liberia

Ghana

Ivory Coast

Togo   Benin

Somalia

Kenya

Dem. Rep. of
the Congo

Tanzania

Atlantic Ocean

Angola

Mozambique

Madagascar

Namibia

N
W   E
S

South Africa

1000km

Portuguese explorers first sailed around the southern tip and up the east coast of Africa in the late fourteenth century. About twenty-five modern African countries now line their route.

Chapter 4

The Europeans Arrive

For nearly two hundred years, from 1095 to 1275, Christian Europe and the Muslim Middle East hammered at one another during a series of bloody religious wars known as the Crusades. These wars, which came in rapid succession, brought death and destruction to a large part of what is today Israel, Lebanon, and Syria. Ending in a stalemate of sorts, the wars left Muslims thoroughly resentful of Europe. They began to interfere with the trade routes between Europe and Asia.

Hoping to go around the Muslims altogether, Europeans began to consider the feasibility of sea routes to the East. Portugal moved first. In 1415, the Portuguese established a base at the port of Ceuta (THAY-oo-tah) on the African coast of the Strait of Gibraltar. Its governor was the royal Prince Henry, who was determined to put Portugal in front of all the other European powers in the race for Asia. He marshaled the kingdom's resources and launched a series of voyages of exploration aimed at finding a way to sail down Africa's west coast, swing around the continent's southern tip, and emerge in the Indian Ocean. From there, it would be on to India and China.

The first of these expeditions arrived in 1419 at Madeira, a group of islands about 350 miles off the west coast of Africa. Madeira would soon become a center of sugar production. By 1443, the Portuguese had established a permanent base on the shores of West Africa. From there, Henry's explorers continued their search for "any harbours where men could enter without peril."[1]

Prince Henry the Navigator saw Portugal's future in Africa. More precisely, he hoped to establish trade routes along the continent's coast that would ultimately lead to the valuable markets of India and China—markets that would make Portugal rich.

They would have to do so without their original sponsor: Henry died in 1460. The Portuguese effort he inaugurated, however, lived on. Henry's countrymen continued their voyages and established settlements and outposts all along the western coast of Africa. At first, Portuguese merchants sought to exploit the lucrative trade in gold and ivory that already flourished in the region. Later, they became the first Europeans to be involved in a practice that already existed in Africa, the buying and selling of slaves. North African Muslims had been importing slaves from the continental interior for centuries, but the people purchased by the Portuguese were destined to leave Africa entirely. These unfortunate captives were sold to planters to work the sugar fields being cultivated on Madeira and other remote locations. There, many would work until they died.

The obvious profit coming out of Africa soon drew the attention of other Europeans. By the time Portuguese explorer Bartolomeu Dias (DEE-az) rounded the Cape of Good Hope in 1487, other European

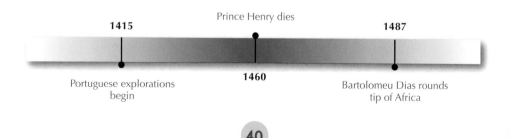

Prince Henry dies

1415

1487

1460

Portuguese explorations begin

Bartolomeu Dias rounds tip of Africa

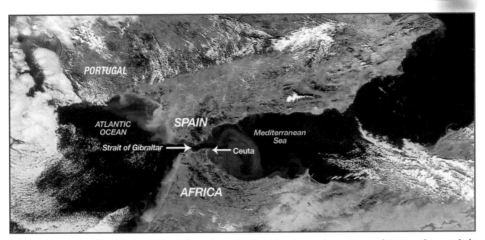

The Strait of Gibraltar, named for the Muslim leader who crossed it in the eighth century, separates Europe from North Africa. It connects the Atlantic Ocean and the Mediterranean Sea. The Portuguese settlement of Ceuta is located on a broad peninsula on the African side.

powers were showing intense interest in Africa. When Vasco da Gama (GAH-mah) sailed into the Indian Ocean in 1498, they realized they had to get into the game before Portugal came to dominate the new routes to Asia. But events conspired to give Portugal almost exclusive control over the sea lanes. Spain, France, and England were distracted through the late fifteenth and early sixteenth centuries by religious wars and the race to set up colonies in the Americas.

With no apparent challengers, Portugal continued to expand its influence in Africa. In many places, this involved the continued development of the slave trade. The kingdom of Kongo, for instance, was losing between 2,000 and 3,000 of its people every year to Portuguese

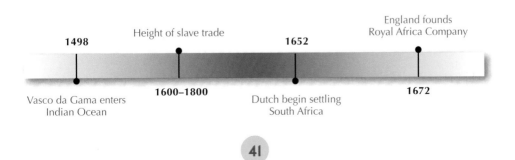

England founds
Royal Africa Company

Height of slave trade

1498   1652

Vasco da Gama enters   1600–1800   Dutch begin settling   1672
Indian Ocean   South Africa

Madeira was one of the first Atlantic islands occupied by the Portuguese at the beginning of their African explorations. Famed for its sugar and later its wine, Madeira today is a popular tourist destination.

slavers by 1526. This prompted the king of Kongo to complain to the Portuguese monarch that ever greater numbers of Africans, "even nobles, sons of nobles, even members of our own family" were being kidnapped by traders who wanted to "sell them to the white people."[2] This hideous trade in human lives only grew larger as the Portuguese began building sugar plantations in Brazil; these plantations demanded slaves to work them.

The Dutch were the first of Portugal's competitors to try to dislodge it from Africa and take over commercial activities there, including the

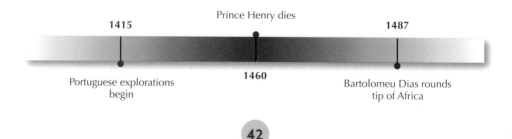

Prince Henry dies

1415

1487

Portuguese explorations
begin

1460

Bartolomeu Dias rounds
tip of Africa

slave trade. In 1602, the Dutch East India Company was founded with the objective of taking the African and Asian markets away from Portugal. Its success was astonishing. Between 1637 and 1642, the Dutch East India Company systematically erased Portuguese influence in the Indian Ocean and seized many of the prime Portuguese outposts on the East African coast. Its counterpart, the Dutch West India Company, did the same thing along the Atlantic coast of Africa.

The Dutch, however, did not hold the places they took for very long. The British and French moved in by the mid-seventeenth century. Both nations set up companies to compete for Africa's trade. The most successful was England's

Europe became obsessed with cane sugar after the Portuguese began cultivating it on the Atlantic islands. For this sweet treat, however, untold thousands of people paid a bitter price. Sugar was produced using slave labor.

Royal Africa Company, founded in 1672. Although it took some interest in other commodities, the slave trade was its real focus. By this time, the market in humans had grown to immense proportions.

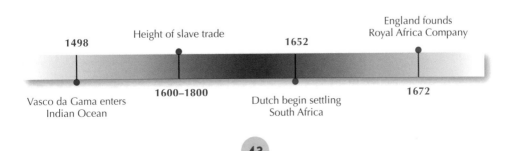

1498
Vasco da Gama enters
Indian Ocean

Height of slave trade
1600–1800

1652
Dutch begin settling
South Africa

England founds
Royal Africa Company
1672

Bartolomeu Dias (left) and Vasco da Gama (right) led the Portuguese march around the Cape of Good Hope and into the Indian Ocean. The two men did for Portugal what Columbus did for Spain: They opened new places, people, and markets to European exploitation.

During the seventeenth century alone, almost two million Africans were enslaved. Over the next century and a half, an additional ten to twenty million men, women, and children would wear chains; a third of them would die in bondage.

Using every available ruse and tactic, African merchant-kings along the coast conspired to feed an almost constant stream of people into the slave markets. They launched small wars designed to take captives, kidnapped entire villages, and even changed their laws to

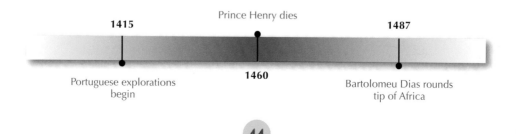

Prince Henry dies

1415

1487

1460

Portuguese explorations begin

Bartolomeu Dias rounds tip of Africa

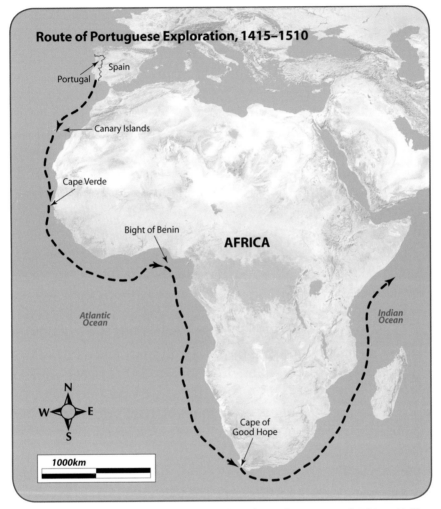

Route of Portuguese Exploration, 1415–1510

Spain

Portugal

Canary Islands

Cape Verde

Bight of Benin

AFRICA

Atlantic Ocean

Indian Ocean

N
W E
S

Cape of Good Hope

1000km

The Portuguese sailed thousands of miles along the coasts of Africa. Unlike the British in the nineteenth century, however, they rarely ventured inland.

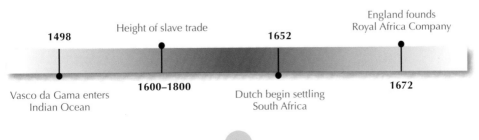

1498

Height of slave trade

1652

England founds Royal Africa Company

1600–1800

Dutch begin settling South Africa

1672

Vasco da Gama enters Indian Ocean

convict more people of crimes and then sell them as slaves. African kings reportedly set slavery as the punishment for just about every crime, "there being an Advantage of such Condemnation . . . in order to get the Benefit of selling the Criminal."[3]

To add to Africa's woes, some Europeans came not just to exploit and go home; they came to stay. Sponsored by the Dutch East India Company, Dutch colonists settled at the Cape of Good Hope in 1652. There they met a diverse array of native peoples, including Khoisan (KOY-sahn) herders, Bantu farmers, and San villagers. These original inhabitants neither feared nor welcomed the newcomers. Fighting soon broke out, but the Dutch settlers had the advantage of modern technology and support from Europe. They displaced South African blacks and built farms on the formerly native lands. White settlement in southern Africa expanded through the seventeenth century.

War between immigrants and natives became commonplace everywhere the whites went. For example, brutal conflicts erupted whenever black Africans came into contact with land-hungry Dutch settlers, otherwise known as Trekboers, who fanned out from the original settlement at the Cape of Good Hope. Bloody raids and fierce battles killed many on both sides. In addition to the slave trade, now supplying unwilling laborers to the farms and plantations of North America, the establishment of permanent European colonies disrupted African life and put intense pressure on the African people.

Hoping to soften this blow, Great Britain took control of South Africa from the Dutch in 1814, but little changed. Even the abolition of slavery throughout the British Empire in 1834 failed to reverse centuries of abuse. Though slavery was withering and dying almost everywhere, new forms of exploitation began replacing it. These concentrated not on Africa's people, but on the material resources that grew from, or lay within, Africa itself.

Dr. Livingstone, I Presume

One of the leading opponents of slavery was British explorer Dr. David Livingstone, who is credited as being among the first Europeans to penetrate into the interior of Africa. In doing so, he opened this previously mysterious land to nineteenth-century colonial powers.

Prior to Livingstone's remarkable journeys through sub-Saharan Africa between 1841 and 1873, few people except the local Africans themselves knew very much about the vast lands that lay between the Congo and Zambezi Rivers. Most Europeans imagined the area to be either a huge desert devoid of human life or an impenetrable complex of mountains.

One popular belief was that the mythical Fountains of Herodotus, the springs from which the headwaters of the Nile flowed, were located somewhere deep in the heart of the area. Until a better understanding of the land and the people of south-central Africa could be gained, nearly a third of the continent was effectively closed to European exploitation.

Livingstone provided the answers to the many questions about the region in a series of expeditions between 1841 and 1856 that made him famous. The intrepid doctor made his way from the coast of modern-day Angola all the way to Mozambique. He set out on another expedition in 1866. When there was no word from him in three years, rumors of his death began circulating and led to one of the great adventure stories of the nineteenth century: the search for Livingstone by the American journalist Henry Morton Stanley.

Carrying the supplies that Stanley believed Livingstone would require if he were indeed alive but lost, the reporter set out to find the good doctor. He did that in 1871, supposedly uttering the greeting, "Doctor Livingstone, I presume." Livingstone did not return to England. He finally met his end, in 1873, in the African heartland that had so intrigued him.

Dr. David Livingstone is carried by native bearers shortly before his death. He was made famous by his travels through the heartland of southern Africa.

King Leopold's Africa, c. 1900

AFRICA

Congo Free
State/Belgian Congo

Atlantic Ocean

1000km

What is today the Democratic Republic of the Congo was once the property of a single man, Belgium's King Leopold II. His personal realm in Africa stretched halfway across the continent.

A Country for a King

For nearly four hundred years, from the first Portuguese exploitations to the abolition of slavery by the British Empire, Africa suffered under the assault of slave traders. Every year, boatloads of kidnapped Africans were shipped abroad. African slaves labored on sugar plantations in Brazil and the West Indies; they toiled in the rice, tobacco, and cotton fields of North America. From the late fifteenth to the mid nineteenth century, Africa was brutally and relentlessly exploited for its human resources, the people who lived and died as slaves.

But the world was changing. Industry was becoming more important. This new order had little use for untrained, degraded agricultural laborers such as slaves. Instead, it needed factory workers. As a result, the business of slavery lost its appeal and began to wither away, assisted by its outright abolition throughout the British Empire in 1834 and its elimination in North America after the bloody Civil War of 1861–1865. Slavery had been recognized as both terrible and unnecessary in an increasingly industrial world.

Slaves were no longer in demand, but raw materials for factories were. Industrialization, designed primarily to produce consumer goods, required large supplies of metals such as iron and copper and other resources that were not abundant in Europe. Rubber and various oils that were essential to manufacturing did not even exist there, so the new industrial powers of Europe had to look elsewhere. Their gaze fell upon Africa.

The brutality of the African slave trade was legendary. The African people endured not only physical abuse, but also the emotional torment of being separated from their families.

By the last quarter of the nineteenth century, European countries were moving to dominate the raw resources of the continent. Germany, having just become a nation in 1871, hoped to quickly catch up in terms of industrialization with the other European states, Great Britain in particular. Africa's resources were crucial to its plans.

Knowing this well, German chancellor Otto von Bismarck moved to put Germany on the map of Africa, or, as he put it, to give his nation

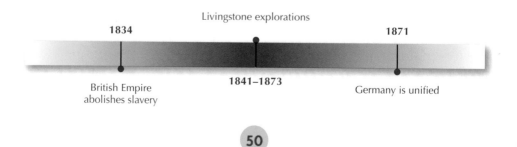

Livingstone explorations

1834

1871

British Empire
abolishes slavery

1841–1873

Germany is unified

a "colonial whirl."[1] In 1884, he invited the great states of Europe, each of which had an interest in Africa, to meet in Berlin to discuss how best to carve up the continent among them. The Berlin Conference didn't establish new colonies in Africa, nor did it define the borders of those already there. Rather, what came out of it was an agreement to abide by a rule known as "effective occupation." According to this doctrine, if a European country actually had enough people to establish its authority in a part of Africa, that nation could claim that place as a colony. What came to be called the Scramble for Africa was on. Whoever got somewhere first could take control of the land, people, and resources they found there.

The harrowing journey from Africa to the Americas was called the Middle Passage. Some estimates put the number of Africans —packed into small, filthy ships—who perished while crossing the Atlantic Ocean in the millions.

The Europeans raced to divide Africa among themselves. One man, however, did not have to run at all to get his share of the continent. King Leopold II of Belgium told one of his royal officials that he was determined to get a share for himself. "I do not want to risk," the king said, "losing a fine chance to secure for ourselves a piece of this magnificent African cake."[2] Set on gobbling up a portion of Africa, Leopold convinced the delegates at the Berlin Conference to give him an

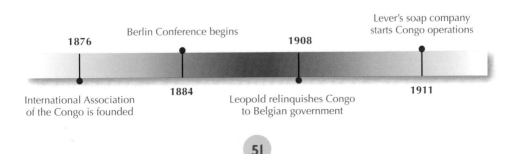

1876 — International Association of the Congo is founded

1884

Berlin Conference begins

1908 — Leopold relinquishes Congo to Belgian government

1911

Lever's soap company starts Congo operations

area in central Africa hundreds of times larger than the kingdom he ruled in Europe.

Founded in 1876, a company known as the International Association of the Congo had been establishing trading posts along the Congo River. The company was secretly controlled by Leopold and funneled most of its profits to him. The Berlin Conference recognized the association's presence as legitimate and granted it all the territory from the Congo River southward to the Zimbabwe Plateau. North of the Congo River, France took over. In effect, the conference gave Leopold his very own African colony to do with as he pleased.

German Chancellor Otto von Bismarck is credited with having founded modern Germany in 1871. He also hosted the conference at which the European nations began the process of dividing Africa among themselves.

Leopold quickly formalized his control, declaring his entire possession to be an entity called the Congo Free State. In reality, it was neither free nor a state. The Free State became a vehicle for Leopold's ambition and greed. Posing as a benevolent European ruler looking out for the best interests of his African subjects, Leopold systematically squeezed the Free State dry of its natural resources, primarily rubber. Rubber was in high demand for use in industrial machinery and as the main component in the tires that turned on bicycles and, by the 1890s,

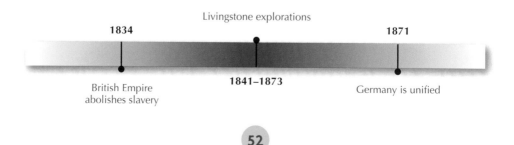

Livingstone explorations

1834

1871

British Empire
abolishes slavery

1841–1873

Germany is unified

on automobiles. Leopold and his associates hoped to acquire and maintain a near monopoly on its production and sale.

Fixated as he was on profit, Leopold turned a blind eye to corruption and rampant abuse in the Congo. His managers in Africa ruthlessly exploited the Congolese people in their desperate search for rubber. Virtual rubber raids became commonplace, as armed expeditions moved through the Congo basin, forcing local villagers to produce and harvest raw rubber for export to Europe. They met resistance with torture and murder. One observer noted how the rubber trade had "reduced the people to a state of utter despair . . . [rubber] is collected by force. The soldiers drive the people into the bush [to harvest it]. . . . If they will not go they are shot down, and their left hands are cut off and taken as trophies."[3]

King Leopold II of Belgium claimed Central Africa as his own. Although many European countries established colonies in Africa, King Leopold was the first (but not the last) individual to found a personal empire there.

The Free State authorities brutalized the people horribly. By the early 1900s, the Congolese began to fight back. A series of uprisings shook the Free State and gained the attention of the public in Europe. Opinion began to turn against Leopold and his bloody enterprise. So did the markets. As alternative sources of rubber became available,

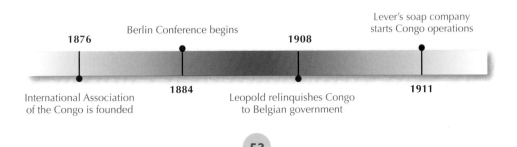

1876 — International Association of the Congo is founded

Berlin Conference begins

1884 — Leopold relinquishes Congo to Belgian government

1908

Lever's soap company starts Congo operations

1911

most significantly in Indonesia, prices for the thick liquid fell dramatically. The reports of abuses and the decline in profitability forced Leopold to give up his domination. He released the Free State from his personal rule in 1908 and turned it over to the government of Belgium, but not before the parliament voted to award Leopold fifty million francs "as a mark of gratitude for his great sacrifices made for the Congo."[4] The place then became a true colony and was renamed the Belgian Congo.

The Great Zimbabwe National Monument, on the Harare Plateau, was at the southern extent of Leopold's territory. Europeans who discovered the ruins in the 1870s did not believe that Africans could have built such a marvelous structure. Indeed, they had—from around 1200 to 1450 CE.

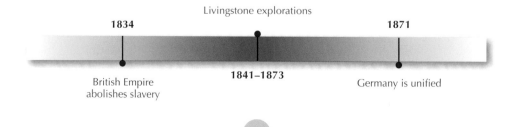

Livingstone explorations

1834	1871

1841–1873

British Empire
abolishes slavery

Germany is unified

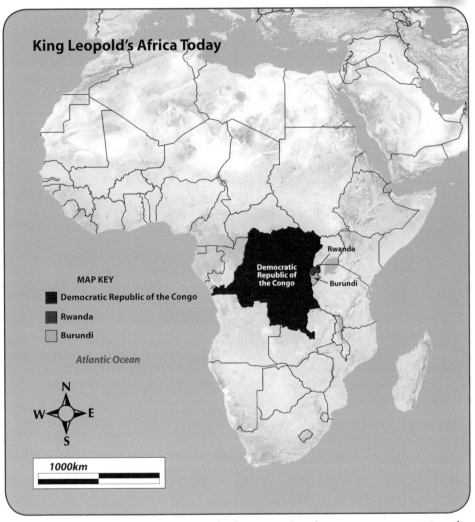

King Leopold's Africa Today

MAP KEY

Democratic Republic of the Congo

Rwanda

Burundi

Atlantic Ocean

N
W   E
S

1000km

King Leopold's private world in Central Africa is today three separate countries: the Democratic Republic of the Congo, Rwanda, and Burundi. Each is an independent nation.

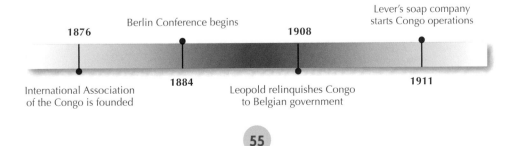

1876

Berlin Conference begins

1908

Lever's soap company starts Congo operations

1884

1911

International Association of the Congo is founded

Leopold relinquishes Congo to Belgian government

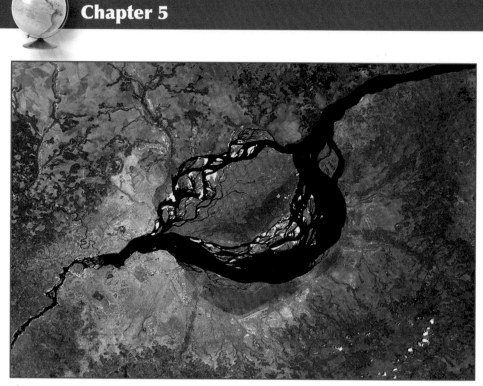

The Congo River, seen from high above the earth, is one of the great waterways of Africa. Snaking through the heart of the continent, it allowed Europeans such as David Livingstone an opportunity to travel deep into what they called the Dark Continent. It also helped in exporting the Congo's natural resources.

Leopold's adventure shaped Congo's future, leaving a legacy of Belgian influence and abuse. It reflected the cruel attitude that many Europeans took toward Africa. The Free State saga typified the Scramble for Africa as nothing else could. Yet Leopold was not the only example of outsized personal greed. To the south of the Congo, a British version of the colonial tyrant had appeared in the form of Cecil Rhodes.

The Congo, William Hesketh Lever, and Soap

In addition to rubber trees, palm trees also abounded in the Congo. They too invited exploitation. For years, cake soaps made from a variety of fats and oils had been gaining in popularity throughout Europe. Merchants everywhere seemed to be carrying these soaps, marketing them under clever brand names to eager consumers.

One of these businessmen was William Hesketh Lever. Born in England in 1851, Lever took over his family's wholesale grocery business in 1874. One of the products he sold was a soap called Lever's Pure Honey. Lever himself did not make the soap, but he labeled it as his own and reaped the profit.

Soon he had made enough money selling groceries to shift his business focus exclusively to soap. By 1888,

An important figure in African history, the soap magnate William Hesketh Lever. Picking up where King Leopold left off, Lever built a business empire by exploiting the palm oil reserves of the Congo.

Lever's business—now named Lever and Company—was turning out 450 tons of soap every week under the brand name Sunlight. Eight years later, Lever introduced Lifebuoy household soap; five years after that, Lux detergent flakes hit the shelves. Lever and his company were becoming rich.

In 1909, an agent of King Leopold approached Lever and told him of the enormous sums of money he could make by using palm oil from the Congo in his products. The rich oil was abundant, Lever was told, and the local workers were already being worked mercilessly by the rubber industry. If Lever's company started operations in the Congo, its owner was assured, it would have access to both raw materials and cheap labor.

Armed with this advice, Lever obtained a concession of nearly two million acres of land in 1911 that allowed him to begin exporting palm oil for use in his soaps. To extract the oil, he relied on some of the same methods perfected by Leopold. Lever's workers were brutalized and worked like slaves. For the next 50 years—well beyond Lever's death in 1925—forced labor would be used in the palm groves of the Congo. Lever thus helped the world cleanse itself through the dirty business of ruthlessly exploiting the people of the Congo.

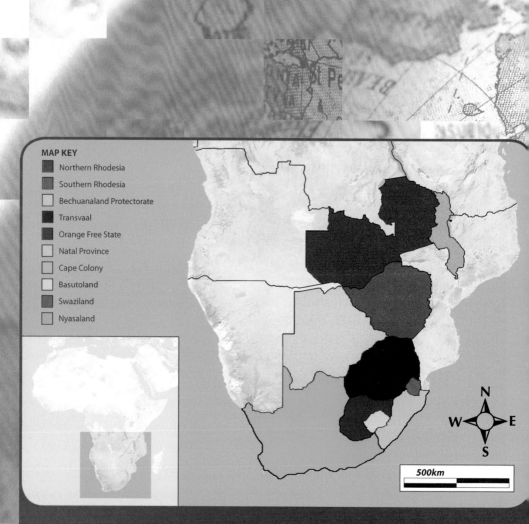

500km

The British carved southern Africa into a patchwork of colonies. Britain subsequently encouraged white migration to the region, giving it perhaps the highest ratio of European-to-African peoples on the continent.

Chapter 6

Cecil Rhodes's Africa

King Leopold's approach to Africa could only be described as predatory. The king leaped on the resources of the Congo and devoured them for his own enrichment. His British counterpart farther south, Cecil Rhodes, did the same thing, but Rhodes was far stealthier. Cecil Rhodes was an adventurer, a mining magnate, and head of the British South Africa Company and the De Beers diamond firm, the two most powerful companies on the African continent in their day. Rhodes, unlike Leopold, was future-oriented. He envisioned an Africa dominated not only by his companies but also more generally by Britain.

"I contend," he once wrote, "that the [British] are the finest race in the world and that the more of the world we inhabit the better it is for the human race. . . . It is our duty to seize every opportunity of acquiring more territory."[1] Rhodes wanted to shape the destiny of southern Africa and leave a lasting imprint on its society and economy. Crafty and intelligent, Rhodes would stop at nothing in his quest to remake Africa in his own way.

Born in 1853, Rhodes emigrated in 1870 from Britain to the Cape Colony, as the British portion of South Africa was known. Shortly after his arrival, he hoped to make his fortune in the diamond fields that had recently been found in territory belonging to the Boer republics of the Transvaal and the Orange Free State. Situated to the north of the Cape Colony, these republics had been founded in the early nineteenth century by the descendants of the early Trekboers. Known by this time simply as Boers, these settlers were fleeing what they considered to be

Cecil Rhodes dominated southern Africa. Shown here astride his horse, Rhodes intended to create a personal empire that, when combined with the larger British Empire, would stretch from the Nile to the Cape of Good Hope.

the "tyranny" of a British empire that had abolished slavery. The Boers wanted to keep their slaves and feared that abolition would eventually lead to equality for blacks.

Both the Transvaal and the Orange Free State were as defensive as they were racist. The Boers hated black Africans to be sure, but they also resented the influx of diamond-hungry foreigners. Yet these *uitlanders* (outlanders), as the Boers called them, brought money, expertise, and an entrepreneurial spirit with them. The Boers, mostly poor farmers, needed all these things desperately. So they tolerated men such as Rhodes, even though they knew well that Rhodes despised them as much as he coveted the diamonds that nature had put in the ground under the Boers' feet.

Rhodes believed the Boers to be a backward people, and he detested their practice of laying heavy taxes on diamond exports. Still, he knew that a great deal of money could be made by paying black

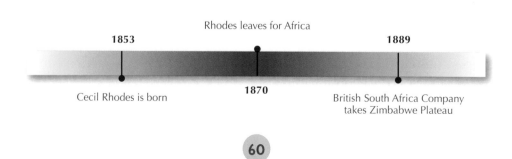

Rhodes leaves for Africa

1853

1889

1870

Cecil Rhodes is born

British South Africa Company takes Zimbabwe Plateau

workers a tiny sum to dig diamonds out of the ground for him. For the time being, Rhodes would put up with his Boer hosts.

In 1871, Rhodes gained a controlling interest in an old mine named for the property on which it sat, the De Beers farm. From there, Rhodes and a handful of partners purchased one mine after another until they had put together an impressive company. Their mines were very

Young Zulus gather in front of a typical diamond mine, owned by the De Beers Company, where they worked long hours in appalling conditions pulling the twinkling gemstones from the ground. Although slavery had ended decades earlier, black Africans were still being exploited at the end of the nineteenth century.

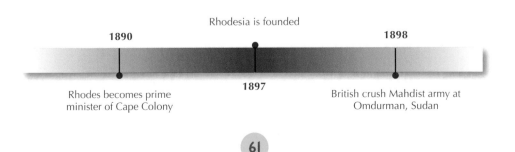

Rhodesia is founded

1890

1898

Rhodes becomes prime
minister of Cape Colony

1897

British crush Mahdist army at
Omdurman, Sudan

successful because they took advantage of the newly pioneered process of using steam machinery to pump groundwater out of the huge diamond pits his workers dug, thus reducing costs and increasing profits. Rhodes soon gained a monopoly of the most lucrative diamond fields, especially those near the city of Kimberley. He brought his holdings together in 1888 and founded a new company, De Beers Consolidated Mines Limited. Cecil Rhodes was on his way to becoming the most powerful man in Africa.

The process of mining diamonds in late-nineteenth-century southern Africa, while still labor intensive, was highly mechanized. State-of-the-art machines, like the diamond washer shown here, made mining more efficient and profitable.

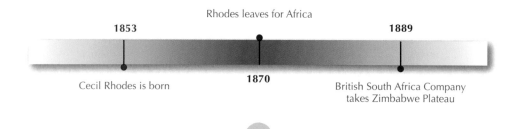

1853

Rhodes leaves for Africa

1889

Cecil Rhodes is born

1870

British South Africa Company takes Zimbabwe Plateau

In 1890, Rhodes became prime minister of the Cape Colony. By then De Beers had made millions of dollars in the midst of the barely controlled confusion of the Scramble for Africa. Rhodes saw his wealth as a tool in his plan to remake Africa in a manner that benefited himself and the British Empire. He dreamed of a British Africa, linked by railroads and telegraph lines, running unbroken from Cairo to Cape Town, regardless of any other Europeans or native Africans who might be in the way. "The railway is my right hand and the telegraph my voice," Rhodes said.[2] Resistance to his vision was unthinkable, Rhodes imagined, but resistance was becoming more common in early colonial Africa.

As the Europeans raced to gobble up as much of Africa as the Berlin Conference allowed, they busily suppressed one native uprising after another. For the British, the greatest threat came from resistance in the ancient land of Nubia. They faced not only a challenge to their colonial rule but also the West's first open combat with the forces of radical Islam.

The Suez Canal had been built through northern Egypt in 1869 to make it easier for Europe to trade with India and China. Its protection was a concern to both Britain and France, which led to their joint financial administration of Egypt in 1879. Three years later, Britain became the sole power when it occupied Egypt. This move put it in direct contact with the Muslim elements in Sudan that saw all Europeans as infidels and invaders.

Chief among these were the followers of Muhammad Ahmad, a mystic who claimed to be the Mahdi (MAH-dee), or Muslim savior. Believing their leader to have been sent by Allah (God) to rescue them from the clutches of the evil Westerners, the Mahdists rose up against

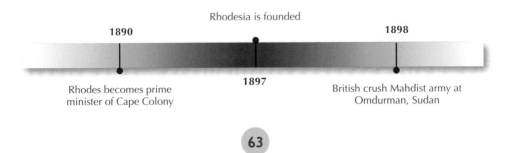

Rhodesia is founded

1890

1898

1897

Rhodes becomes prime minister of Cape Colony

British crush Mahdist army at Omdurman, Sudan

The Suez Canal links the Mediterranean Sea and the Indian Ocean through the Red Sea. Dug out from the desert sands of the Sinai Peninsula, the canal allowed Europeans, especially the British, to create vast commercial networks that spanned the globe.

the British in 1885 and destroyed the Anglo-Egyptian garrison stationed at the city of Khartoum (kar-TOOM). Ironically, the British commander at Khartoum was General Charles Gordon, one of Rhodes's personal friends. "I am sorry I was not with him,"[3] Rhodes said sadly after hearing of Gordon's death. Though the Mahdi died soon after the Khartoum uprising, the British and the Mahdists fought one battle after another for more than a decade. Though they were outnumbered, the British crushed the Mahdist army at Omdurman, in Sudan, in 1898 by employing artillery and the recently invented machine gun.

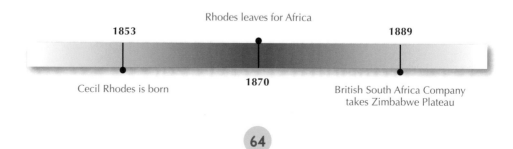

Rhodes leaves for Africa

1853   1889

Cecil Rhodes is born   1870   British South Africa Company
                                                        takes Zimbabwe Plateau

Cecil Rhodes hoped to avoid this kind of unrest and bloodshed as he made Africa safe for exploitation by De Beers and the new British South Africa Company (BSAC), a firm set up in 1889 by Rhodes mainly in the hopes of finding as-yet-undiscovered riches on the Zimbabwe Plateau. Lying north of the Boer republics, the plateau, Rhodes believed, held large quantities of gold. The gold mines of southern Africa, like the diamond fields, lay almost exclusively within the

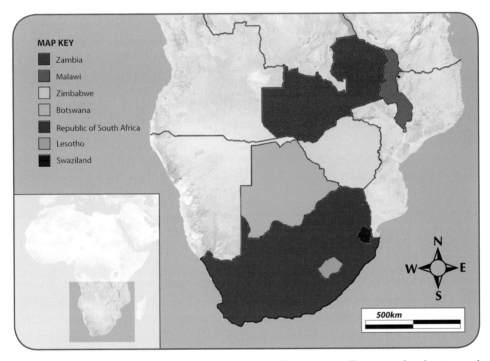

MAP KEY
- Zambia
- Malawi
- Zimbabwe
- Botswana
- Republic of South Africa
- Lesotho
- Swaziland

Nineteenth-century Europeans knew southern Africa as a collection of colonies and private business holdings. Today, the region is home to some of Africa's most vibrant, and often most troubled, nations.

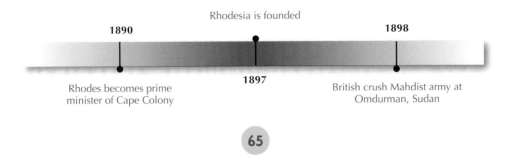

Rhodes is founded

1890

1898

1897

Rhodes becomes prime minister of Cape Colony

British crush Mahdist army at Omdurman, Sudan

borders of the Boer republics. If he could get control of an independent source of gold, Rhodes thought, he might be able to break the Boer stranglehold on access to the riches of the south.

Rhodes had heard rumors of hidden Zimbabwean gold mines that had not been worked for centuries, so he raced to seize them. Recognizing the fact that the local people would not welcome greedy white men, Rhodes used deception to get his way. BSAC representatives fooled the ruler of the largest African group into signing an agreement that allowed the company to take "whatever action they consider necessary" to mine for gold.[4] The action Rhodes took was to send a column of heavily armed miners to the Zimbabwe Plateau. The men found little gold but a great deal of hatred and fierce resistance. Eventually, British troops from the Cape Colony had to be dispatched to the north. It took almost ten years of sporadic fighting to quell the violence.

Cecil Rhodes was close to having the personal African empire he had always dreamed of. De Beers Consolidated effectively controlled the Cape Colony, while the BSAC ruled the land that had been renamed Rhodesia in honor of its conqueror. "Has anyone else had a country called after their name?" Rhodes exclaimed, "Now I don't care what they do to me!"[5] (Rhodesia would remain the company's property until 1911, when the southern part became the crown colony of Southern Rhodesia. The northern portion was transferred to imperial administration in 1924 as the British protectorate of Northern Rhodesia.)

With the Zimbabwe region and the Cape Colony firmly in hand, Rhodes had the Boer republics squeezed between his corporate holdings. If he could eliminate the Boers and their taxes, Rhodes knew he would likely receive the exclusive rights to the gold and diamonds of southern Africa. Although the Boer leaders did not know it, the crafty Briton had already begun plotting against them.

Cecil Rhodes

Cecil Rhodes was born in Hertfordshire, England, on July 5, 1853. His father was the Reverend Francis Rhodes, a religious man responsible for the tiny rural parish of St. Michael's. Rhodes's mother was a sturdy young woman named Louisa Peacock Rhodes, her husband's second wife.

As a boy, Cecil lived a conflicted life. His mother was warm and loving, but his father was a distant man who rarely expressed his feelings. At home, the Reverend Rhodes enforced a strict discipline: The children were discouraged from idle conversation and—especially the boys—kept hard at work. He gave them little time for play and exploration of the world around them.

As a student, Cecil excelled at history and geography. Books and maps allowed him to exercise his spirit of adventure, at least in his imagination. The world opened up to him at school and offered the hope of a life far away from his overbearing father.

Cecil Rhodes left an enduring mark on southern Africa. His name, however, disappeared from the map in 1980, when the country of Southern Rhodesia became modern Zimbabwe.

The Reverend Rhodes wanted his son to become a minister, but Cecil had other ideas. Using the need to recover from a bout of sickness as an excuse, Cecil pressured his parents to send him abroad to recuperate. An older brother had already left for South Africa, and Cecil longed to go there too. His parents eventually gave in, and Cecil left for South Africa in June 1870. He was only seventeen years old.

Once in South Africa, Rhodes decided to make a living farming cotton with his brother. He quickly realized, however, that the real money and excitement lay in the diamond fields. In November 1871, the eager young man staked his first claim near Kimberley, at the site of an old farm named De Beers. A piece of Africa now belonged to Rhodes, and Rhodes would now forever belong to Africa. While he was on a visit to England later in his life, an acquaintance asked him how long he planned to stay in the country of his birth. Rhodes shot back, "Not a moment longer than I can help."[6]

South Africa During the Boer War

MAP KEY
- Cape Colony
- Orange Free State
- Transvaal
- Natal Province

Pretoria
(Transvaal capital)

Kimberley

Bloemfontein
(Orange Free
State capital)

Cape Town

N
W E
S

400km

Long before South Africa was a single political state, it was three independent entities. The British Cape Colony was bordered by the Transvaal Republic and the Orange Free State, countries ruled by white descendants of the first Europeans to settle in the region.

A White War in a Black Land

Rhodes's success in the north renewed his interest in gaining control of the rest of southern Africa. The Cape Colony was already essentially his, and the last serious black challenge to white exploitation in the region—the Zulu War of 1879—had been turned back. Only one hurdle remained for Rhodes—stubborn Boer resistance to outside interference in the economies of the Transvaal and Orange Free State. The Boer republics were fiercely independent and firmly in charge of some of the most promising gold and diamond mining territory in the world. Rhodes was determined to break that hold and make the entire southern reaches of Africa his through De Beers and the British South Africa Company.

His first attempt failed miserably. Late in 1895, Rhodes concocted a clumsy and ill-conceived scheme to foment rebellion among the *uitlanders* in the Transvaal. Drawing on his covert invasion of Zimbabwe, Rhodes armed a company of BSAC workers and put them under the command of Dr. Leander Jameson. Jameson's mission was to enter the Transvaal and wait for the mostly British foreigners to join him in overthrowing the government of Transvaal president Paul Kruger. No such uprising took place, Jameson was captured in 1896, and the Boers were alerted to Rhodes's intentions. The embarrassed Rhodes resigned as prime minister in South Africa's government.

The British government, however, gave its official support to Rhodes's plan to overcome the Boers and demanded concessions from the Transvaal. Despite the failure of the Jameson raid, Kruger was told,

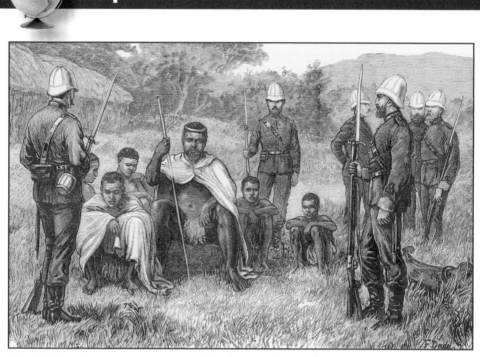

The Zulu king Cetawayo was captured by the British near the end of the Anglo-Zulu War. He was the last king of an independent Zulu nation.

foreigners must be given the right to exploit his country's mineral resources with the least amount of Boer interference. To emphasize their point, the British sent troops to the northern borders of the Cape Colony in 1899. Explaining the move, British Colonial Secretary Joseph Chamberlain said bluntly, "Our supremacy in South Africa, and our existence as a great power in the world are involved."[1]

Left with only one alternative, Kruger declared war on Britain in October 1899; the Orange Free State quickly did likewise. Almost as soon as the war broke out, the combatants announced their agree-

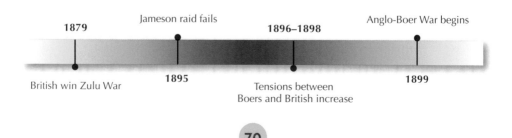

| 1879 | Jameson raid fails | 1896–1898 | Anglo-Boer War begins |

British win Zulu War   1895   1899
                      Tensions between
                      Boers and British increase

The British raid into the Transvaal in 1895 was a disaster. Its leader, Dr. Leander Jameson, shown above after being captured by the Boers, had been given the dubious task of fomenting a rebellion among the Boer Republic's British residents.

ment that this would be a white man's war. They wouldn't involve Africans in the fighting. Officially forbidden from participating on either side, black South Africans became spectators to a bloody contest that would determine the future of their white neighbors and ultimately their own.

Within days, Boer *kommandos*, small units of mounted fighters, invaded the Cape Colony and the neighboring province of Natal. They scored one victory after another over the British, who were poorly led and ill-prepared for combat against their elusive and tenacious foe. The Boers were capable of fighting both large battles and also small hit-and-run actions. They proved to be skilled marksmen who were well motivated and well equipped: They carried the most modern and lethal firearm of the day, the German-made Mauser Model 98 bolt-action rifle.

Moving southward and fanning out to the west, the Boers laid siege to cities such as Mafeking, Ladysmith, and Kimberley, where Cecil Rhodes himself was staying at the time. Along with 500 British soldiers and 50,000 civilians, Rhodes remained a virtual Boer prisoner

Boer guerrilla campaign

1900

1902

1901–1902

British take Orange Free State and Transvaal

Cecil Rhodes dies

British colonial secretary Joseph Chamberlain. The British vastly underestimated Boer determination to remain free of British influence. Perhaps no one miscalculated the degree of Boer resistance more than he.

for the next four months. The inability of British troops to free Kimberley infuriated Rhodes. "Is it reasonable," he fumed, "to expect something better than that a large British Army should remain inactive in the presence of eight or ten thousand peasant soldiers?"[2]

Time and again, the Boers bested the imperial troops facing them. The week of December 10 to 15, 1899, for instance, saw so many major British defeats that the London newspapers called it "Black Week." Nevertheless, when Queen Victoria was told that the Boers might be winning, she replied, "We are not interested in the possibilities of defeat; they do not exist."[3]

The queen's determination reinvigorated the British. In January 1900, new commanders took over on the British side, and significant numbers of regular troops arrived from England; the tide of the war turned against the Boers. By February, the British were advancing on every front, and large Boer forces began surrendering. Kimberley was relieved on February 15, freeing Rhodes, the man who had helped provoke the war in the first place.

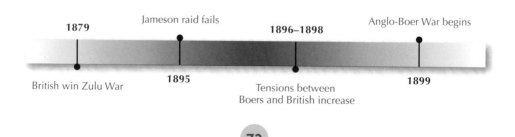

1879 — British win Zulu War

Jameson raid fails — 1895

1896–1898 — Tensions between Boers and British increase

Anglo-Boer War begins — 1899

A group of *kommandos* in a typically defiant pose. Tough, well armed, and hardened by life on a farm, Boer soldiers, known as *kommandos*, surprised the British with their military skills and resilience.

By the late spring of 1900, the defeat of the Boer republics was certain. The Orange Free State surrendered to the British in May and became an imperial colony. That summer, President Paul Kruger fled into exile, and the Transvaal gave up. It was annexed by Great Britain in September. Rhodes and his British sponsors had removed the last political obstacle to their power in white South Africa.

Boer guerrilla campaign

1900

1902

British take Orange Free State and Transvaal

1901–1902

Cecil Rhodes dies

A Scottish regiment, in their distinctive kilts, after the Battle of Magersfontein in the Orange Free State. The British sent the best army in the world to South Africa during the Great Boer War.

Militarily, however, the fight was not over. Boer *kommandos* remained in the field. With no country to serve, these Boers took it upon themselves to resist the might of Great Britain. Employing guerrilla tactics against their enemies, they relentlessly attacked supply trains, remote army outposts, and isolated garrisons. Having nowhere and everywhere to go, the Boers struck hard and then simply melted away into the vast grasslands and mountains of their homeland. Often, British soldiers neither saw nor heard their attackers. When British

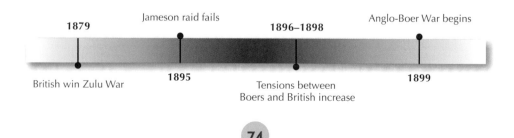

1879

Jameson raid fails

1896–1898

Anglo-Boer War begins

British win Zulu War

1895

Tensions between
Boers and British increase

1899

patrols tried to hunt down small groups of Boers, their quarry vanished.

Frustrated by their inability to engage the men who were tormenting them, the British retaliated with a deliberate policy of using Boer families as hostages. Hoping to isolate the Boer fighting men by cutting them off from their supplies and loved ones, the British burned

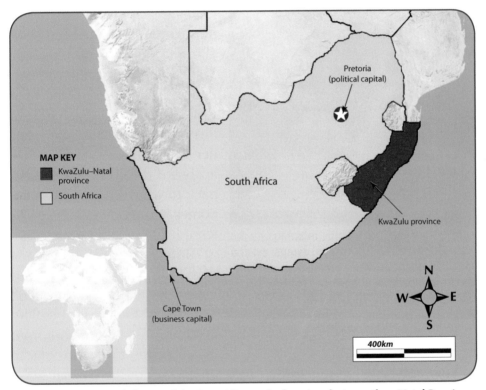

MAP KEY
- KwaZulu–Natal province
- South Africa

Pretoria (political capital)

South Africa

KwaZulu province

Cape Town (business capital)

N
W ◆ E
S

400km

Some of the hardest fighting of the Boer War took place in what was then Natal Province. Today it is known as KwaZulu-Natal, a province of the republic of South Africa.

Boer guerrilla campaign

1900

1902

British take Orange Free State and Transvaal

1901–1902

Cecil Rhodes dies

Long before they were made infamous by the Nazi Germans, concentration camps existed in South Africa. Used to relocate Boer civilians, the camps became notorious for their harsh conditions and the high death rates among the women and children interned there.

Boer farms and herded the unfortunate women and children into concentration camps. Thousands eventually died from malnutrition and disease in the squalid conditions there.

The Boers, fearing for their relatives and unable to defeat the British, finally ended their guerrilla campaign in May 1902. By a strange coincidence, Cecil Rhodes, the man who had done so much to start the Anglo-Boer War, died earlier that year. The Boers accepted British rule and went back to what remained of their homes to rebuild their shattered lives.

British domination in Africa now extended from Egypt and Sudan in the north to the Cape Colony in the south. Indigenous resistance—whether from the Mahdists in Sudan, blacks in Rhodesia, or whites in South Africa—had been broken. What stood as perhaps the earliest serious attempts at African liberation had failed. Yet colonial rule, while still secure, had been shaken. It would fall to pieces after the European colonial powers took it upon themselves to fight two world wars, the results of which profoundly altered the history of Africa.

Blacks in White Wars

One of the most difficult decisions faced by whites on both sides during the American Civil War was integrating tens of thousands of blacks into their war efforts. During the Boer War in South Africa, the combatants faced a somewhat similar dilemma. Two white armies were fighting for supremacy in a black land. Briton and Boer alike were minorities in South Africa. The role of black South Africans in the war thus became an important issue.

At first, the British and their Boer opponents agreed that blacks would stay out of the contest. Both sides were equally racist and believed that the danger posed by armed blacks was far greater than the threat of defeat. No matter who won the war, it was believed, white people would still rule South Africa.

Giving blacks guns and encouraging them to kill whites, therefore, was inherently counterproductive. After the whites were finished shooting each other, whoever won would have to face an armed black majority that had grown accustomed to fighting against white rulers. When the British violated this unwritten rule by arming some blacks, a Boer general angrily accused them of having "committed an enormous act of wickedness" and demanded that his enemies "disarm [their] blacks and thereby act the part of a white man in a white man's war."[4]

Reality, however, intervened. Neither the British nor the Boers could sustain combat operations very long without black support. Boer farmers who went off to fight relied on black labor to grow the food that kept them going. Fast-moving Boer armies used black porters to transport vital supplies and equipment from one battlefield to another.

The British used black workers as well. They went one step further and, as noted above, armed a number of blacks. Most of these troops were stationed in fortified blockhouses designed to keep Boer guerrillas out of areas that had been captured by imperial troops. Others were given more aggressive roles and saw actual combat against the Boers.

Battle-toughened Boers were also determined racists. They believed that their war against Britain was a war for white liberation and, in the end, white supremacy in South Africa.

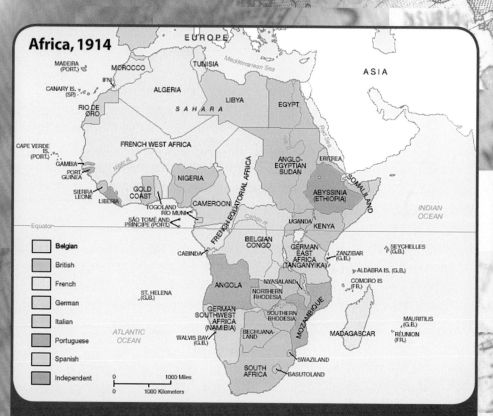

Africa, 1914

EUROPE

MADEIRA (PORT.)
MOROCCO
IFNI
CANARY IS. (SP.)
RIO DE ORO
TUNISIA
Mediterranean Sea
ALGERIA
LIBYA
EGYPT
SAHARA
ASIA

CAPE VERDE IS. (PORT.)
FRENCH WEST AFRICA
Niger R.
GAMBIA
PORT. GUINEA
SIERRA LEONE
LIBERIA
GOLD COAST
TOGOLAND
RIO MUNI
SÃO TOMÉ AND PRINCIPE (PORT.)
NIGERIA
CAMEROON
ANGLO-EGYPTIAN SUDAN
ERITREA
SOMALILAND
Red Sea
ABYSSINIA (ETHIOPIA)
INDIAN OCEAN

Equator

FRENCH EQUATORIAL AFRICA
Congo R.
UGANDA
KENYA

CABINDA
BELGIAN CONGO
GERMAN EAST AFRICA (TANGANYIKA)
ZANZIBAR (G.B.)
SEYCHELLES (G.B.)
ALDABRA IS. (G.B.)
COMORO IS. (FR.)

ST. HELENA (G.B.)
ANGOLA
NYASALAND
NORTHERN RHODESIA
MOZAMBIQUE
MAURITIUS (G.B.)
RÉUNION (FR.)

ATLANTIC OCEAN
GERMAN SOUTHWEST AFRICA (NAMIBIA)
WALVIS BAY (G.B.)
SOUTHERN RHODESIA
BECHUANA-LAND
MADAGASCAR

SOUTH AFRICA
SWAZILAND
BASUTOLAND

Legend:
- Belgian
- British
- French
- German
- Italian
- Portuguese
- Spanish
- Independent

0 — 1000 Miles
0 — 1000 Kilometers

European states and kingdoms systematically pulled Africa apart in the nineteenth century. The map above shows the extent of their division of the continent by the beginning of World War I.

Chapter 8

The World Fights in Africa

Africa remained firmly in Europe's colonial clutches through the first decade of the twentieth century. Some resistance was offered here and there, such as the Herero Uprising against the Germans in South West Africa (present-day Namibia) from 1904 to 1907, but European domination of the continent was virtually total. Perhaps more important, the rationale for colonization was unquestioned: Europe ruled Africa for its own benefit, as well as for the good of the benighted Africans. Certainly, it was argued, Europe took what natural resources it needed from Africa, but it gave back the modern benefits of Christianity, civilization, enlightenment, and technology. Words such as *self-determination* and *independence for native peoples* were not part of the colonial vocabulary.

A savage war that began in 1914 would soon change that fact. After years of antagonism among the continent's great powers, and war plans that locked each country into alliances, World War I erupted. It would be the single largest bloodletting in human history. Millions of men would die on the battlefields of France and Belgium; hundreds of thousands would fall in the Middle East or drown at sea as the Allies (Britain, France, Russia, Italy, and—starting in April 1917—the United States) grappled with the Central Powers (Germany, Austria-Hungary, Bulgaria, and Turkey). Fighting broke out wherever the world's empires had interests at stake.

That included Africa. Soon after the mutual declarations of war that put armies in motion in Europe, the African colonies held by the

The Herero Uprising resulted in one of history's worst examples of colonial savagery. For three years, black Africans in what is now Angola fought a desperate battle against the Germans. Only by resorting to mass murder and the wholesale destruction of farms and villages could the Germans defeat their African enemies.

combatants felt the hand of war upon them. Nearly one million African men found themselves in one uniform or another. The British refused to allow black soldiers to fight against whites. Black men could serve in Africa or the Middle East, the British announced, "but *not* against German troops in Europe."[1] The French had no such reluctance. Over 450,000 black Africans fought in the trenches alongside white Frenchmen against the Germans.

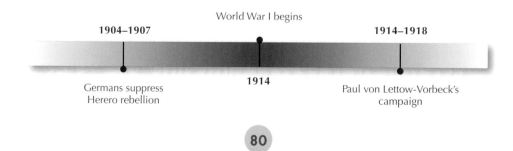

World War I begins

1904–1907   1914–1918

1914

Germans suppress Herero rebellion

Paul von Lettow-Vorbeck's campaign

To escape the Germans, who methodically devastated the Herero lands during the rebellion, some Herero crossed the desolate Omaheke desert. Many perished on the way, and the rest nearly starved.

In Africa itself, British and French forces almost immediately invaded the German colonies of Togo and Cameroon. Togo was quickly overrun, but the Cameroon campaign lasted nearly two years before ending with an Allied victory. Acting as part of the British Commonwealth, South African troops charged into German South West Africa soon after the outbreak of the war and occupied it in 1915.

The fiercest combat took place in German East Africa, what is today Tanzania. Hoping to replicate Allied successes in the west, the British

1915

Belgian troops join
British in attacks

1918

South African troops occupy
South West Africa

1916

World War I ends

stormed in from British East Africa (modern Kenya). By 1916, the Belgians joined the British, attacking from bases in the Belgian Congo. A South African force from Rhodesia came in as well. Neither side could gain an advantage and fighting continued until the armistice in November 1918 ended the First World War. In January 1919, the former

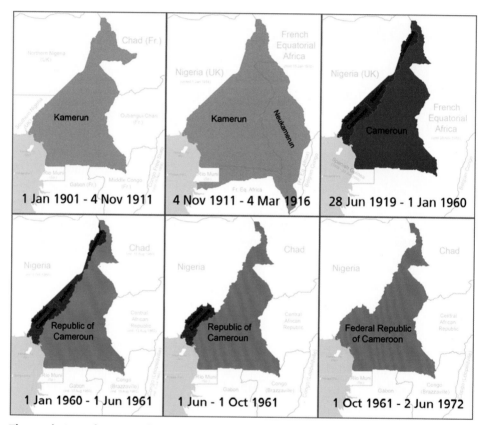

1 Jan 1901 - 4 Nov 1911	**4 Nov 1911 - 4 Mar 1916**	**28 Jun 1919 - 1 Jan 1960**
1 Jan 1960 - 1 Jun 1961	**1 Jun - 1 Oct 1961**	**1 Oct 1961 - 2 Jun 1972**

The evolution of many independent states in Africa was a long and arduous process. The example of Cameroon is shown in this chart.

World War I begins

1904–1907   1914–1918

1914

Germans suppress   Paul von Lettow-Vorbeck's
Herero rebellion   campaign

combatants met at the palace of Versailles outside of Paris and signed a treaty that formalized the defeat of the Central Powers. More important for Africa, the treaty stripped Germany of its colonies and distributed them to the victors.

There was more. Infused with the rhetoric of American president Woodrow Wilson, World War I took on a meaning and purpose that the Europeans had not prepared for. Wilson labeled the conflict as a war for freedom, a "people's war . . . waged against . . . the enemies of liberty."[2] He saw imperialism as the cause of the war and believed that

World War I ended officially with the Treaty of Versailles. The peace document that stopped one of history's bloodiest wars was signed at the palace.

Belgian troops join British in attacks

1915

1918

1916

South African troops occupy South West Africa

World War I ends

only liberty could prevent another one. The president challenged the imperial states of Europe to begin programs of self-determination aimed at creating nation-states out of their possessions in Europe.

Infected with the racism common in his day, he was not thinking of Africa. Nevertheless, his words reached Africa and led some Africans to ask why they should not determine the future of their own continent.

Racism was part of the answer. Self-determination, it seemed, applied only to white people, who deemed themselves as superior to blacks. Such thinking might have held, but an even more destructive war broke out.

Tensions in Europe had begun growing not long after the Treaty of Versailles. In the mid-1930s, Adolf Hitler and his Nazi Party transformed Germany from a defeated empire into a racist, nationalist state, possessing a dangerous military. Benito Mussolini and his Fascist Party had already taken over Italy by then. Seeking to build an Italian empire, Mussolini's government made its designs on Africa clear when it invaded Ethiopia in 1935.

World War II began in September 1939 when the Germans invaded Poland. The fighting soon spread to Africa. The Italians, part of the so-called Axis alliance with Germany and Japan, attacked British Somaliland from Ethiopia, and then attacked Egypt from Libya, which they had held before World War I. The British counterattacked, pushing the Italians out of Ethiopia and driving them back into Libya. The famous German *Afrika Korps* soon joined the fighting in North Africa, the scene of nearly all the battles of World War II in Africa.

The absence of battles, however, did not mean that Africa south of the Sahara was not impacted. The Allies drew heavily on the military

Italy invades Ethiopia

1919

1939

Germany loses African colonies

1935

World War II begins

manpower of the continent. Britain conscripted forces from Nigeria, Gold Coast, Sierra Leone, British East Africa, Nyasaland, and the Rhodesias. A total of 374,000 black Africans served in British forces. The French drafted 160,000 Africans from its colonies. The Belgians employed troops from the Belgian Congo. South Africa provided over 210,000 men to the British armed forces, one third of whom were unarmed black laborers. African soldiers fought not only in North Africa but also in Italy and France, and in the Pacific against the Japanese.

World War II in North Africa cost hundreds of thousands of lives. Among the dead were many German soldiers, who were buried in desert graveyards.

1941

German-Italian forces leave Africa

1945

Battles in North Africa begin

1943

World War II ends; Pan-African Congress demands decolonization

General Bernard Law Montgomery leads an armored advance against the Germans in the fall of 1942. Montgomery was the overall British commander in North Africa during some of the toughest fighting there.

The real importance of World War II in Africa came when the conflict ended in 1945. Much as the justification for World War I had planted the notion of self-determination in the heads of many Africans, the antiracist rhetoric of World War II undercut the basic premise of colonialism. At the Pan-African Congress in 1945—the fifth of a series of meetings that dated back to 1919—African sentiment was made clear.

"We are determined to be free," the delegates proclaimed. "We demand for Black Africa autonomy and independence."[3] If racism, as practiced by the Germans and Japanese, had been immoral and intolerable, many Africans argued, then using race as an excuse for colonial domination was just as evil. A war that revealed the horrors of racism—the Nazi effort to murder the Jews of Europe and the Japanese atrocities against peoples they deemed racially inferior—could not end without calling into question all forms of hatred based on ethnicity or skin color. The seeds of liberation had sprouted in Africa.

The Germans in East Africa

The North African exploits of the famed World War II German general Erwin Rommel, who commanded the *Afrika Korps*, are well known. Yet few people today remember Colonel Paul von Lettow-Vorbeck, the German officer who kept Allied armies in East Africa at bay for four years during World War I. When the war broke out, von Lettow-Vorbeck commanded a minuscule force of 218 German officers and just over 2,500 African troops known as askaris (ahs-KAR-eez).

Colonel Paul von Lettow-Vorbeck

Not only was his command small, it was also far beyond the reach of reinforcements and communication with Germany. Von Lettow-Vorbeck and his men would be on their own. Still, von Lettow-Vorbeck very early took the war to the enemy.

In early November 1914, von Lettow-Vorbeck's contingent defeated a far larger British invasion force that sought to drive the Germans from what is today Tanzania. Outnumbered eight to one, the German officers and their askaris killed or wounded several thousand British soldiers.

As the fighting progressed and his enemies numbered up to 100,000 men at times, it became clear to von Lettow-Vorbeck—whose little army never numbered more than 12,000—that he couldn't win against such overwhelming odds. He decided that all he could do was not lose. German armies were at that moment struggling to defeat the Allies in Europe. If he could keep the British and Belgians busy in East Africa, he figured that he might be able to help turn the tide in Europe.

He began practicing guerrilla warfare. Covering countless miles of ground on foot, the German force used stealth and hit-and-run tactics to pin down their enemy. Von Lettow-Vorbeck led his soldiers on a series of campaigns fought across an area ranging from Kenya to Rhodesia, which he invaded just before the war ended in 1918. This skilled and determined officer was widely respected by friend and foe alike. He later became an opponent of the Nazis during the 1930s and 1940s. Paul von Lettow-Vorbeck lived a quiet life after World War II and died in 1964.

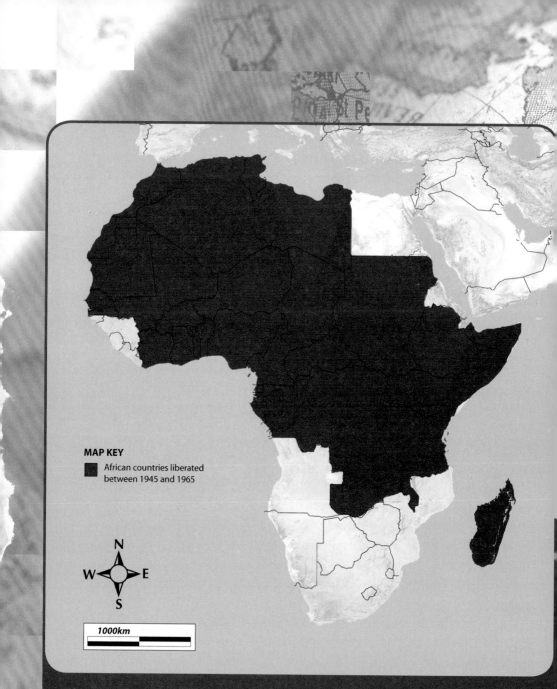

MAP KEY

■ African countries liberated
between 1945 and 1965

1000km

The Europeans dominated and exploited Africa for generations. When the continent finally did gain liberation, it came in abundance. Nearly three-fourths of its countries became independent between 1945 and 1965.

Chapter 9

Liberation and Beyond

World War II generated ideas about racial equality and national liberation that directly impacted Africa. As early as 1941, the British and Americans promised to restore "sovereign rights and self-determination to those who have been forcibly deprived of them."[1] in the famous Atlantic Charter. The war had been fought to destroy the notion that one people could rule over another simply on the basis of imagined racial superiority.

The war also swept away the assumption that exploitation of human and natural resources could be justified in terms of a colonial power's material advancement. The Nazi goal of global domination and the Japanese idea that the island empire should rule all of Asia were deemed to be immoral. After the war, many voices called for an equal application of the term *immoral*. *All* attempts to govern against the will of the governed, it was said, were wrong.

The new rhetoric of freedom after 1945 had many sources. The European democracies began to recognize the hypocrisy of holding colonial empires while talking about nationalism and liberty. The United States portrayed itself as a vehicle for guiding the entire world into a better day. The Soviet Union, the People's Republic of China, and communist parties around the globe talked of a worldwide revolution to throw off the chains of imperialism and colonialism. The language of liberation was being spoken everywhere.

The days of colonialism were ending in practical terms as well. After nearly six years of war, Europe was totally exhausted. The battles

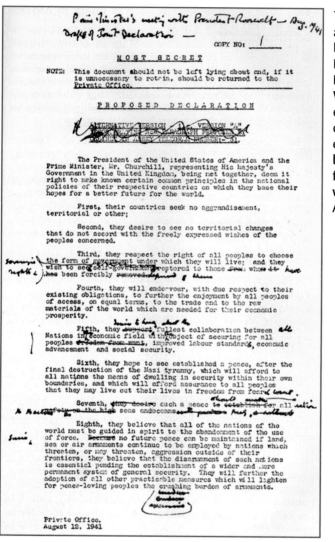

The Atlantic Charter was a joint declaration made by U.S. President Franklin Delano Roosevelt and British Prime Minister Winston Churchill, who edited this draft. The charter envisioned an entirely new global order based on independence for all the nations of the world, including those in Africa.

1954–1962

Algerian war
of independence

1956

Sudan independent

1960

Belgian Congo and some West
African countries independent

Congo dictatorship begins

1961

that had raged across the continent shattered its infrastructure. Roads, factories, farms—sometimes nearly entire cities—had been destroyed. Tens of millions of people were dead. The European militaries were battered and, in the cases of Germany and Italy, utterly broken. National treasuries in almost every country in Europe had been drained or seriously depleted. The old colonial powers, in short, were physically and financially incapable of maintaining their overseas empires.

The colonial zeal that had fired people like King Leopold and Cecil Rhodes was extinguished. Throughout Africa, the process of decolonization began. While it proceeded relatively smoothly in French West Africa, there were some conflicts. As the French withdrew from North

Kenyan herdsmen in traditional dress. Kenya declared its independence in the 1960s.

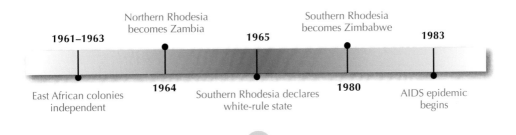

	Northern Rhodesia becomes Zambia		Southern Rhodesia becomes Zimbabwe	1983
1961–1963		1965		
East African colonies independent	1964	Southern Rhodesia declares white-rule state	1980	AIDS epidemic begins

Africa, for example, they engaged in a bitter war with Algerian nationalists that lasted from 1954 to 1962, when the French finally let go of their old colony. Portugal, in the 1960s and 1970s, fought wars in Angola and Mozambique before giving both countries their independence.

The British also found themselves grasping for the last straws of colonial rule in Africa. In British East Africa, a resistance group known as the Mau Mau battled British soldiers until 1955. Their struggle laid

Rebel gunman ride through the Darfur region of Sudan in 2006. The process of African liberation and subsequent nation-building was and remains very difficult. Decades after gaining its freedom, Sudan suffers from poverty and violence.

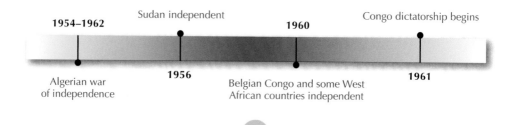

1954–1962

Sudan independent

1960

Congo dictatorship begins

1956

1961

Algerian war of independence

Belgian Congo and some West African countries independent

the foundation for the state of Kenya, which gained independence in 1963.

Other areas under British rule acquired nationhood with significantly less bloodshed. Gold Coast (Ghana, 1957), Nigeria (1960), Sierra Leone (1961), Tanganyika (Tanzania, 1961), Uganda (1962), and Gambia (1965) came into existence with minimal turmoil. Even Sudan, the home of ancient Nubia, experienced its worst violence during the years after its liberation in 1956, as northern Muslims and southern Christians contended for power.

The Belgian Congo and southern Africa experienced altogether different paths to independence. Northern and Southern Rhodesia had large white populations that felt threatened by the entire notion of liberation because it almost certainly meant black rule. In copper-rich Northern Rhodesia, the white minority hoped to gain autonomy without giving power to the black majority. They failed. When independence came in 1964, the country was turned over to a black government, which renamed the country Zambia.

The whites of Southern Rhodesia had no intention of giving their black neighbors such authority. Of all the "Europeans of Central Africa," it was said, "those of Southern Rhodesia have the worst antipathy towards Africans."[2] Led by a fiery racist politician, Ian Smith, Southern Rhodesia's whites declared their own independence in 1965.

The newly independent white government immediately set about trying to destroy its black political opponents, namely the Zimbabwe African National Union (ZANU), which was headed by Robert Mugabe. From 1965 to 1980, a vicious racial war shredded Rhodesian society and brought the country to the brink of economic ruin. Both sides finally recognized the futility of the conflict and agreed to

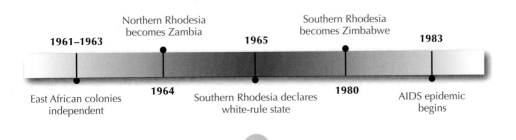

| 1961–1963 | Northern Rhodesia becomes Zambia | 1965 | Southern Rhodesia becomes Zimbabwe | 1983 |

East African colonies independent   1964   Southern Rhodesia declares white-rule state   1980   AIDS epidemic begins

The father of modern Zimbabwe moved from being a liberator to a dictator in just over twenty-five years. Today, President Robert Mugabe is blamed for many of his county's problems, including economic stagnation and white flight from Zimbabwe's farmlands.

elections in 1980. Mugabe's ZANU won, and the black-ruled nation of Zimbabwe was born.

The Belgian Congo also followed a bloody path out from under colonial rule. Granted its independence in 1960, the Congo rapidly descended into political chaos. The government of Prime Minister Patrice Lumumba, who once bragged that the Congolese would "show the whole world what the black man can do when he is allowed to work in freedom,"[3] was shaken by an army mutiny followed by a rebellion in the copper-mining province of Katanga. Rioting erupted and lawlessness became the order of the day. As more than 25,000 Belgians fled the country, taking their expertise and wealth with them, 10,000 Belgian troops were flown in.

Lumumba, confused and fearing the recolonization of his homeland, turned to the Soviet Union (modern Russia) for help. When the Soviets responded positively, the United States became convinced that they were trying to create the foundation for a communist empire in Africa.

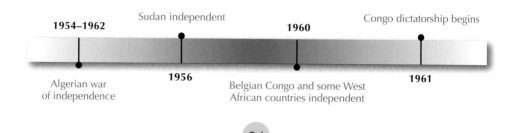

| 1954–1962 | Sudan independent | 1960 | Congo dictatorship begins |

Algerian war of independence — 1956 — Belgian Congo and some West African countries independent — 1961

Perhaps no African leader is associated more closely with the hopes and dreams of liberation than the former Prime Minister of the Congo, Patrice Lumumba. Lumumba represented what Africans thought the future would bring: democracy and prosperity. He was ousted in a U.S.-backed coup in 1960 and later assassinated with the knowledge of the CIA.

Within months, American spies were preparing to depose Lumumba and replace him with someone more friendly to U.S. interests. On the evening of September 14, 1960, a Congolese army commanded by Colonel Joseph Mobutu took power with full American backing. Lumumba was arrested and taken to Katanga, where he was murdered the following January by Congolese and Belgian mercenaries. Mobutu consolidated his hold on the Congo and in 1971 renamed it the Republic of Zaire (zy-EER). He simultaneously renamed himself Mobutu Sese Seko ("All-Powerful Warrior") and ruled Zaire as a dictator for nearly three decades before being overthrown. Known thereafter as the Democratic Republic of the Congo, the country continued to experience repeated bouts of political violence.

By the 1990s, the colonial burden had been lifted from Africa. The only remaining outpost of white colonialism was South Africa. Whites there refused to give up their stranglehold on power even as the rest of

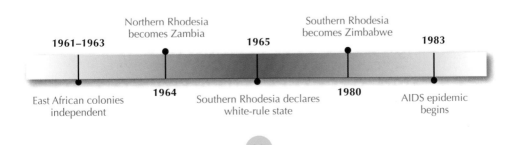

Northern Rhodesia becomes Zambia

Southern Rhodesia becomes Zimbabwe

1961–1963   1965   1983

1964   1980

East African colonies independent

Southern Rhodesia declares white-rule state

AIDS epidemic begins

Joseph Mobutu, shown here in his general's uniform, changed his name to Mobutu Sese Seko in an effort to legitimize his takeover of the Congo in 1960. His career from that point was characterized by oppression and corruption.

the continent enjoyed the fruits of liberty. For decades, they had resisted calls for change coming mainly from the African National Congress (ANC), a group that fought for an end to white rule and the laws that upheld it. Known as apartheid legislation, these laws mandated not only the separation of whites, blacks, and coloreds (people of mixed race), but also the legal subordination of South Africa's black majority. Under these laws, blacks who opposed the minority government were imprisoned and sometimes killed. Perhaps the most famous of the prisoners of conscience held by the South African government was ANC president Nelson Mandela. When he was freed in 1990 after twenty-seven years in jail, it became apparent to everyone that colonialism was dying in its last bastion. Four years later, South Africa's first free and fair election—one that included black voters—resulted in a black government and the striking down of apartheid. The country's first black president was none other than Nelson Mandela.

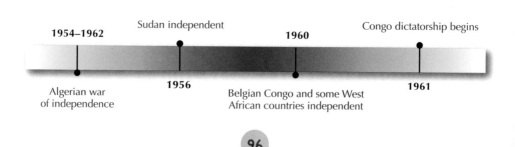

1954–1962
Algerian war of independence

Sudan independent

1956

1960

Belgian Congo and some West African countries independent

Congo dictatorship begins

1961

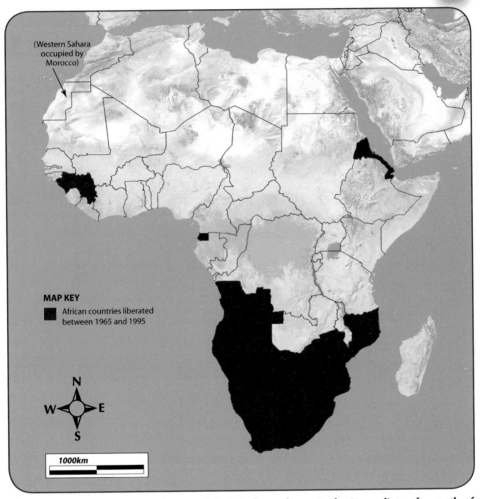

(Western Sahara occupied by Morocco)

MAP KEY

African countries liberated between 1965 and 1995

N
W E
S

1000km

Although most African nations gained their independence in the immediate aftermath of World War II, others took a bit longer to assert their freedom. The map above shows those countries that became independent after 1965.

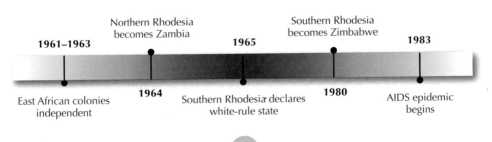

Northern Rhodesia becomes Zambia

Southern Rhodesia becomes Zimbabwe

1961–1963

1965

1983

East African colonies independent

1964

Southern Rhodesia declares white-rule state

1980

AIDS epidemic begins

The liberation of Africa from white rule was personified in Nelson Mandela. After spending decades in prison for his belief that South Africa's black majority should rule the land, Mandela became the country's first black president not long after his release.

With the ending of white rule in South Africa, the last vestige of European domination was erased from the continent. Africa had been liberated and Africans were set to face a promising yet troubled future. Pandemic diseases, civil wars, famine, and political upheaval shook the continent as it entered the twenty-first century. Millions of people were dying of HIV/AIDS; southern Africa was the hardest hit. Poverty and malnutrition were rampant. Ethnic tensions led to bloodshed in the Darfur region of Sudan in 2003.

But across Africa, the continent's people redoubled their efforts to take control of their own destinies. Nation after nation attacked a suite of problems ranging from environmental destruction to the illegal trade in diamonds. Popular movements dedicated to ensuring that the exploitation of Africa's resources benefited common people sprang up in many places. Thus, at the dawn of the new millennium, Africa was well on its way to once again being for Africans.

AIDS and Africa

Of all the problems facing Africa in the early twenty-first century, none needs to be more urgently addressed than the AIDS epidemic. AIDS (Acquired Immunodeficiency Syndrome) is caused by the Human Immunodeficiency Virus (HIV) and is always fatal. The disease, however, can take ten years or longer to kill those infected with it, which means that they suffer the painful and debilitating effects of the collapse of their immune systems long before they die.

Electron-micrograph image of cell producing HIV

By 2007, over twenty-five million Africans were either carrying HIV in their blood or dying from full-blown AIDS. Seventeen million people in Africa had died since 1983, and each day another 6,600 people were following them to the grave. Worse, for the thousands who die, many more become infected. Even the human costs of slavery pale beside the AIDS crisis in its negative impact on an entire continent.

Not only do the victims of the illness suffer terribly, but so do their local and national communities. People who are desperately sick cannot work very hard or very long. As a result, agriculture in many parts of Africa is declining. This leads to food shortages, hunger, and malnutrition. Economic life comes to a virtual standstill when a disease that leaves people too weak to perform even basic types of labor hobbles the workforce.

Parents who die leave behind children who must be cared for at the expense of other family members. This increases the risk that more people will fall into poverty. Children whose parents have died but who do not have relatives or extended families to help them become true orphans. They must either fend for themselves in a harsh and dangerous world or become dependent upon governments that already have trouble caring for their people. In 2007, twelve million African children were in that predicament. For these and many other reasons, AIDS presents perhaps the greatest threat Africa has ever faced.

AIDS orphans in sub-Saharan Africa

Timeline

BCE

c. 2695–c.2195 Egypt is ruled by the pharaohs who built the pyramids during a period known as the Old Kingdom.

c. 2500 The Great Pyramids of Giza are built.

c. 1535–c.1050 The New Kingdom pharaohs rule Egypt and conquer Nubia.

1050 The New Kingdom collapses, allowing the Nubians to form their own state, known as Kush.

c. 730 Kush armies overrun Egypt.

c. 700 The Nubians begin building pyramids.

667 The Assyrians invade and conquer Kushite Egypt.

CE

350 Meroe collapses.

c. 800 Aksum collapses, ending the influence of Nubia and its successors in northeastern Africa.

c. 900 The kingdom of Ghana begins its rise to become the preeminent power in West Africa.

c. 1100 Internal problems bring Ghana down.

c. 1200 The empire of Mali replaces Ghana as the dominant West African state.

1312–1337 King Mansa Musa rules Mali.

1400 Great Zimbabwe dominates the region between the Zambezi and Limpopo rivers; Mali's power comes to an end; Songhay confederation begins to form in Mali.

1415 Portuguese seafarers set sail on Europe's first voyages of exploration.

1460 Prince Henry "the Navigator," sponsor of Portuguese exploration, dies.

1487 Bartolomeu Dias sails around the southern tip of Africa.

1498 Vasco da Gama sails into the Indian Ocean, opening a new trade route to Asia, just six years after Columbus reaches America.

1591 Songhay, the successor to the empire of Mali, is brought down by invaders from Morocco.

1600–1800 The slave trade is at its height.

1652 The Dutch establish a settlement at the Cape of Good Hope in South Africa.

1672 England founds Royal Africa Company.

1834	The British Empire abolishes slavery.
1841	David Livingstone begins explorations of southern Africa.
1853	Cecil Rhodes is born.
1869	The Suez Canal is built in Egypt.
1870	Rhodes leaves England for Africa, where he starts mining the next year.
1871	Germany becomes a unified country.
1873	Livingstone dies.
1879	The British win the Zulu War, ending native resistance in South Africa.
1884	The Berlin Conference opens in the German capital; over the next year, the European powers carve up Africa among themselves.
1888	Rhodes's British South Africa Company gains access to Zimbabwe Plateau.
1890	Cecil Rhodes and De Beers diamond company dominate British South Africa; Rhodes becomes prime minister of Cape Colony.
1895	The Jameson Raid provokes conflict in South Africa.
1896–1899	Tensions grow between the Boer republics and the British.
1897	Rhodesia is founded and named after Cecil Rhodes; it remains the property of Rhodes's British South Africa Company until 1911.
1898	British crush Mahdist army at Omdurman, Sudan.
1899	The Anglo-Boer War begins; the early months see Boer success.
1900	The British regain the initiative in Boer War; Orange Free State surrenders in May; Transvaal is annexed in September.
1901–1902	Boers conduct guerilla campaign; atrocities on both sides.
1902	Cecil Rhodes dies; the Anglo-Boer War ends.
1904–1907	The Germans suppress Herero rebellion in South West Africa.
1908	King Leopold II is compelled to give the Congo to the Belgian government.
1911	Lever's company sets up operations in the Congo.
1914	World War I begins; British and French seize German colonies in West Africa; fighting that lasts throughout the war begins in East Africa.

1915	South African troops occupy German South West Africa.
1918	World War I ends.
1919	The Versailles peace conference strips Germany of its African colonies.
1924	The upper portion of Rhodesia becomes separate country called Northern Rhodesia.
1935	Italy invades Ethopia.
1939	World War II begins.
1940	Fighting in North Africa begins.
1941	Ethiopia is liberated from Italy.
1943	The final German and Italian forces are driven out of Africa.
1945	World War II ends; the Pan-African Congress demands African decolonization.
1954	The Algerian war of independence begins and lasts until 1962.
1956	Sudan becomes independent.
1960	Several West African countries gain independence; Belgian Congo is freed.
1961	A military coup brings down democratic government of Congo; dictatorship begins.
1961–1963	Several East African colonies gain independence.
1964	Northern Rhodesia comes under black rule and is renamed Zambia. Lake Nasser forms after construction of Aswan High Dam.
1965	Southern Rhodesia's whites declare their colony to be an independent white-ruled state.
1980	Southern Rhodesia becomes Zimbabwe after a long civil war ends in black rule.
1983	The AIDS epidemic strikes Africa.
1988	Timbuktu becomes a World Cultural Heritage Site.
2001	Whites are pressured to leave Zimbabwe.
2003	The Nubian pyramids are recognized as world cultural treasures.
2006	Elections are held in the Democratic Republic of the Congo.
2007	The black government of Zimbabwe encourages the return of whites.

Chapter 1. Strange Things in Strange Places

1. "Pyramids in Sudan—Nubia," http://www.crystalinks.com/pyrsudan.html

2. John Iliffe, *Africans: A History of a Continent* (New York: Cambridge University Press, 1995), p. 28.

3. "Eye on Africa: Bamba's Concession Speech," http//dizolele.com/?p=159

4. Christopher Thompson, "Zimbabwe Poised to Welcome Back White Farmers," *Guardian Unlimited*, January 3, 2007, http://www.guardian.co.uk/zimbabwe/article/0,,1982144,00.html

5. Rosemary Ekosso, "Zimbabwe: White Lies, Black Victims," http://www.africaspeaks.com/articles/2006/0308.html

6. Danna Harman, "Hearts Heavy, Whites Feeling Driven From Africa," *Christian Science Monitor*, February 2, 2003, http://www.csmonitor.com/2003/0227/p01s03–woaf.html

7. Martin Gough, "Exiles Happy at Return to the Fray," http://news.bbc.co.uk/sport2/hi/cricket/3897249.stm

Chapter 2. From Nubia to Kush

1. Lorna Oakes and Lucia Gahlin, *Ancient Egypt* (New York: Hermes House, 2002), p. 216.

2. Ian Shaw, editor, *The Oxford History of Egypt* (New York: Oxford University Press, 2000), p. 356.

3. A.T. Olmstead, *History of Assyria* (Chicago: University of Chicago Press, 1951), p. 645.

4. John Reader, *Africa: A Biography of the Continent* (New York: Vintage Books, 1997), p. 216.

Chapter 3. Africa for Africans

1. John Reader, *Africa: A Biography of the Continent* (New York: Vintage Books, 1997), p. 286.

2. Kevin Shillington, *History of Africa* (New York: St. Martin's Press, 1989), p. 99.

Chapter 4. The Europeans Arrive

1. J.D. Fage, *A History of Africa* (New York: Routledge, 1995), p. 222.

2. John Iliffe, *Africans: A History of a Continent* (New York: Cambridge University Press, 1995), p. 130.

3. Ibid., p. 133.

Chapter 5. A Country for a King

1. Thomas Pakenham, *The Scramble for Africa: The White Man's Conquest of the Dark Continent from 1876 to 1912* (New York: Random House, 1991), p. xxiii.

2. Adam Hochschild, *King Leopold's Ghost: A Story of Greed,*

Terror, and Heroism in Colonial Africa (Boston: Houghton Mifflin, 1998), p. 58.

3. Kevin Shillington, *History of Africa* (New York: St. Martin's Press, 1989), pp. 334–335.

4. Hochschild, p. 259.

Chapter 6. Cecil Rhodes's Africa

1. Brian Roberts, *Cecil Rhodes: Flawed Colossus* (New York: W.W. Norton and Company, 1987), p. 1.

2. Ibid., p. 148.

3. Ibid., p. 52.

4. Kevin Shillington, *History of Africa* (New York: St. Martin's Press, 1989), p. 323.

5. Roberts, p. 207.

6. Ibid., p. 1.

Chapter 7. A White War in a Black Land

1. Denis Judd and Keith Surridge, *The Boer War* (New York: Palgrave Macmilllan, 2002), p. 46.

2. Ibid., p. 148.

3. Byron Farwell, *The Great Anglo-Boer War* (New York: W.W. Norton and Company, 1976), p. 142.

4. Brian Smith, "BBC Radio Retrospective on the Anglo-Boer War, 1899–1902." http://www.wsws.org/articles/1999/sep1999/boer–s29.shtml

Chapter 8. The World Fights in Africa

1. John Reader, *Africa: A Biography of the Continent* (New York: Vintage Books, 1997), p. 607.

2. Lloyd C. Gardner, *Safe for Democracy: The Anglo-American Response to Revolution, 1913–1923* (New York: Oxford University Press, 1984), p. 1.

3. Reader, p. 643.

Chapter 9. Liberation and Beyond

1. John Reader, *Africa: A Biography of the Continent* (New York: Vintage Books, 1997), p. 639.

2. Kevin Shillington, *History of Africa* (New York: St. Martin's Press, 1989), p. 396.

3. Reader, p. 657.

Books

Dudley, William, editor. *Africa: Opposing Viewpoints*. San Diego: Greenhaven Press, 2000.

Habeeb, William Mark. *Africa: Facts and Figures*. Philadelphia: Mason Crest Publishers, 2005.

Ibazebo, Isimene. *Explorations into Africa*. Philadelphia: Chelsea House Publishers, 2001.

Mann, Kenny. *Ghana, Mali, Songhay: The Western Sudan*. Parsippany, New Jersey: Dillon Press, 1996.

Murray, Jocelyn. *Africa*. New York: Facts on File, 1990.

Shuter, Jane. *Ancient West African Kingdoms*. Chicago: Heinemann Library, 2003.

Works Consulted

Ekosso, Rosemary. "Zimbabwe: White Lies, Black Victims." http://www.africaspeaks.com/articles/2006/0308.html

"Eye on Africa: Bamba's Concession Speech." http://dizolele.com/?p=159

Fage, J.D. *A History of Africa*. New York: Routledge, 1995.

Farwell, Byron. *The Great Anglo-Boer War*. New York: W.W. Norton and Company, 1976.

Gardner, Lloyd C. *Safe for Democracy: The Anglo-American Response to Revolution, 1913–1923*. New York: Oxford University Press, 1984.

Gough, Martin. "Exiles Happy at Return to the Fray." http://news.bbc.co.uk/sport2/hi/cricket/3897249.stm

Harman, Danna. "Hearts Heavy, Whites Feeling Driven From Africa." *Christian Science Monitor*, February 2, 2003. http://www.csmonitor.com/2003/0227/p01s03–woaf.html

Hochschild, Adam. *King Leopold's Ghost: A Story of Greed, Terror, and Heroism in Colonial Africa*. Boston: Houghton Mifflin, 1998.

Iliffe, John. *Africans: A History of a Continent*. New York: Cambridge University Press, 1995.

Judd, Dennis, and Keith Surridge. *The Boer War*. New York: Palgrave Macmilllan, 2002.

Oakes, Lorna, and Lucia Gahlin. *Ancient Egypt*. New York: Hermes House, 2002.

Olmstead, A.T. *History of Assyria*. Chicago: University of Chicago Press, 1951.

Pakenham, Thomas. *The Scramble for Africa: The White Man's Conquest of the Dark Continent from 1876 to 1912*. New York: Random House, 1991.

"Pyramids in Sudan—Nubia." http://www.crystalinks.com/pyrsudan.html

Reader, John. *Africa: A Biography of the Continent*. New York: Vintage Books, 1997.

Roberts, Brian. *Cecil Rhodes: Flawed Colossus*. New York: W.W. Norton and Company, 1987.

Shaw, Ian, editor. *The Oxford History of Egypt*. New York: Oxford University Press, 2000.

Shillington, Kevin. *History of Africa*. New York: St. Martin's Press, 1989.

Smith, Brian. "BBC Radio Retrospective on the Anglo-Boer War, 1899–1902." http://www.wsws.org/articles/1999/sep1999/boer–s29.shtml

Thompson, Christopher. "Zimbabwe Poised to Welcome Back White Farmers." *Guardian Unlimited*, January 3, 2007. http://www.guardian.co.uk/zimbabwe/article/0,,1982144,00.html

On the Internet
Africa: Just for Kids
http://www.calacademy.org/exhibits/africa/kids.htm
Kidipede—History for Kids
http://www.historyforkids.org/learn/africa/
PBS: Africa for Kids
http://pbskids.org/africa/

abhorrence (ub-HOR-uns)—Extreme dislike.

antechamber (AN-tee-chaym-bur)—A room that leads to another, larger room.

antipathy (an-TIH-puh-thee)—Strong dislike.

apartheid (ah-PAR-tyd)—A system of racial separation used in South Africa.

autonomy (aw-TAH-noh-mee)—Independence.

benevolent (beh-NEH-vuh-lunt)—Willing to do good things for others.

benighted (beh-NY-tid)—Ignorant; not well-informed.

chancellor (CHAN-suh-lur)—A political leader similar to a prime minister.

confiscate (KON-fis-kayt)—To take something without giving anything in return.

covert (koh-VERT)—Secret.

cricket (KRIH-ket)—An English game that resembles baseball.

entrepreneurial (on-treh-preh-NUR-ee-ul)—Having to do with starting and running a business.

hieroglyphics (hy-roh-GLIH-fiks)—A form of picture writing used in ancient Egypt.

immune system (ih-MYOON sis-tum)—The part of a body that fights off sickness.

indigenous (in-DIH-jih-nus)—Something that is native to a particular place.

interloper (IN-ter-loh-per)—An uninvited person or intruder.

magnate (MAG-nayt)—A rich or important businessperson.

mercenaries (MUR-suh-nayr-eez)—Soldiers who are hired to fight for a country other than their own.

monotheistic (mah-noh-thee-ISS-tik)—Having a belief in only one god.

obelisks (AH-buh-lisks)—Four-sided pillars topped with a small pyramid.

pandemic (pan-DEH-mik)—Extremely widespread.

predatory (PREH-duh-tor-ee)—Plundering, destructive.

resin (REH-zin)—A type of tree sap that hardens like plastic.

rhetoric (REH-tor-ik)—The art of speaking effectively; the use of insincere or misleading language.

sphinx (SFINKS)—An imaginary animal that has the head of a human and the body of a lion.

suite (SWEET)—A group of things; a collection.

Index

About the Author

John Davenport holds a Ph.D. in History from the University of Connecticut and is the author of numerous books on subjects ranging from biography to historical geography. His published works include a history of the Nuremburg war crimes trials and a biography of the medieval Muslim leader Saladin. Davenport teaches social studies at Corte Madera Middle School in Portola Valley, California. He lives in San Carlos, California, with his wife, Jennifer, and his two sons, William and Andrew.